THE SKYE TRAIL

First published 2010 by Mountain Media Productions Ltd

Mountain Media Productions Ltd
Old Glen Road
Newtonmore
Inverness-shire PH20 1EB

www.mountain-media.co.uk

Text by Cameron McNeish for Mountain Media Productions Ltd

Photography by Richard Else for Mountain Media Productions Ltd

Maps drawn by Gregor McNeish

Design and layout by Gregor McNeish

Set in 11.5pt Aldine Light / Trajan

Printed by Butler Tanner & Dennis Ltd, Frome, Somerset

ISBN-13: 978-0-9562957-1-2

Contact details, accommodation and travel information are correct at the time of going to press. Significant changes will be posted on **www.mountain-media.co.uk.**

The **Leave No Trace** principles are reproduced by kind permission of the Leave No Trace Center for Outdoor Ethics, Boulder, CO, USA.

The maps in this book are intended as a rough guide and should not be used for navigational purposes in the field.

THE SKYE TRAIL

A journey through the Isle of Skye

CAMERON MCNEISH AND RICHARD ELSE

Looking down on Camasunary Bay

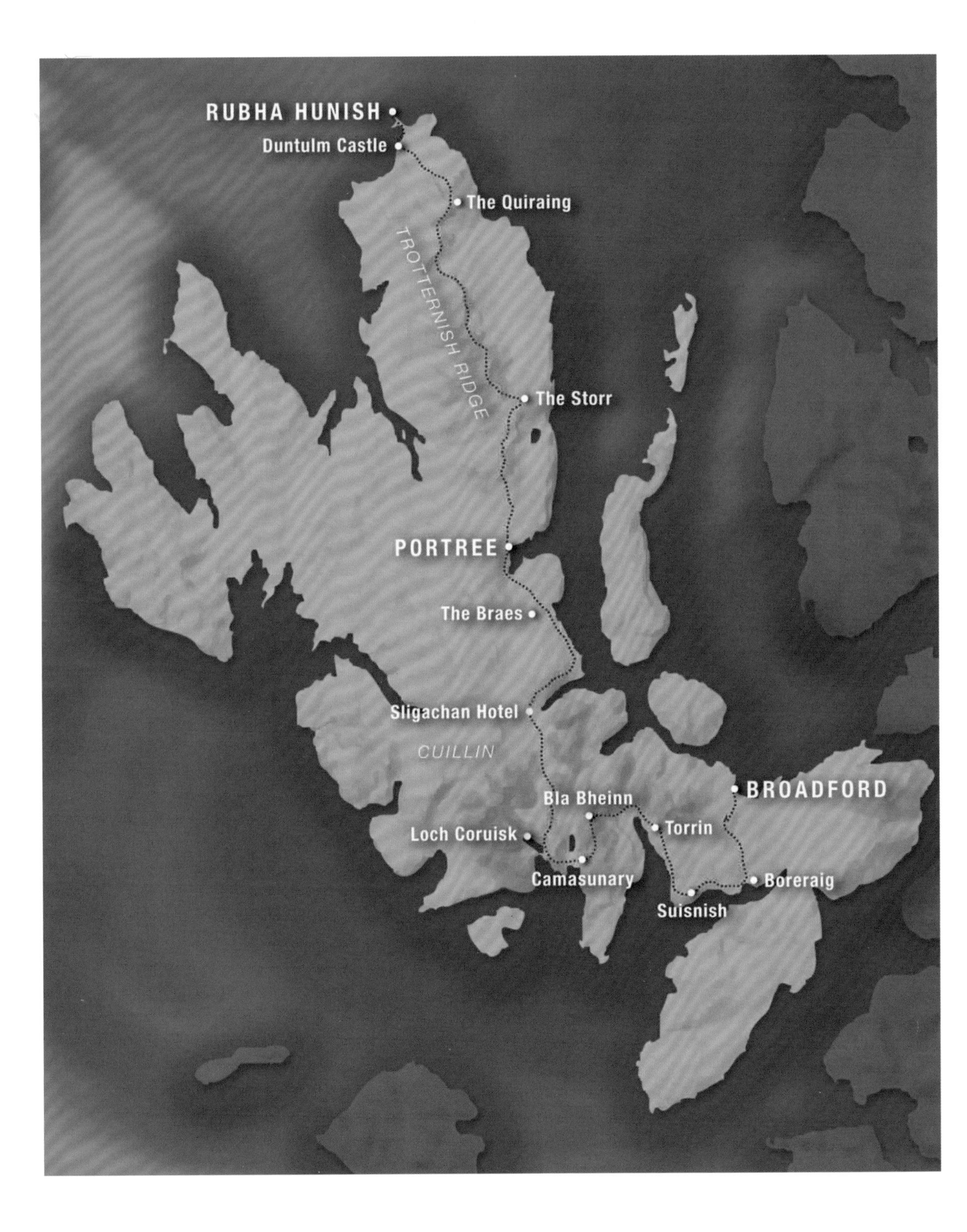
RUBHA HUNISH
Duntulm Castle
The Quiraing
TROTTERNISH RIDGE
The Storr
PORTREE
The Braes
Sligachan Hotel
CUILLIN
BROADFORD
Bla Bheinn
Torrin
Loch Coruisk
Camasunary
Boreraig
Suisnish

Contents

Looking towards Staffin from The Quiraing

Acknowledgements

We are both indebted to everyone who helped us produce this book and the television programme it came from, especially all those kindly people who served us latte and cappuccinos in a whole variety of cafes, tea shops and hotels up and down the length of Skye.

Particular thanks must go to David Harron, our long-enduring editor at Television Sport, BBC Scotland, who once again has given us unfailing encouragement and support despite being soaked to the skin as we went through our plans with him one very wet day on Creag Dhubh near Newtonmore. Sincere thanks are also due to our Commissioning Editor at BBC Scotland, Ewan Angus who, although not a hillwalker himself, has backed adventure sports in Scotland to such a degree that he should be awarded a medal himself. Or perhaps a pair of walking boots would be more appropriate.

Once again Dominic Scott has proved to be a cameraman of exceptional ability and we are both delighted that he can be so easily bribed by an endless supply of lattes. His camerawork provided the basis for a great film and we were always impressed by his ability to vanish into midge-infested evenings just to get that extra bit of footage.

Paul Tattersall and John Lyall once again came along as our safety officers and continually encouraged us by their patience, good humour and ability to carry awkward tripods. Their companionship was appreciated by everyone involved.

A good television programme, and a good book, depends largely on the people you are filming or writing about and once again Lady Luck, and some very good research, provided us with a bunch of terrific interviewees. Many thanks to Karen Hardie, Pascal Riveaux, John Phillips, Lorne Nicolson, Meg Bateman, Cailean Maclean, Alastair MacPherson and David Craig. Warm thanks are also due to everyone who looked after us so well at the Sligachan Inn. After some long days working in the rain it was a real pleasure to return to such a comfortable and hospitable bolthole. Warm thanks are also due to Roger Smith for his patience and editing skills.

Gina McNeish once again looked after Cameron's every need on their recce walk between Trotternish and Elgol and Margaret Wicks kept up her solid record of producing another excellent television programme as well as organising all our filming, interviews and movements on Skye. Thanks are also due to James and Liv Else for their musical and production contributions to the television programme and to Gregor McNeish whose design skills have ensured another high quality book. As the authors age considerably with every production it's good to know that we have offspring of such talent and ability. At least we've done something right somewhere along the line…

Cameron McNeish and Richard Else, *Newtonmore, August 2010*

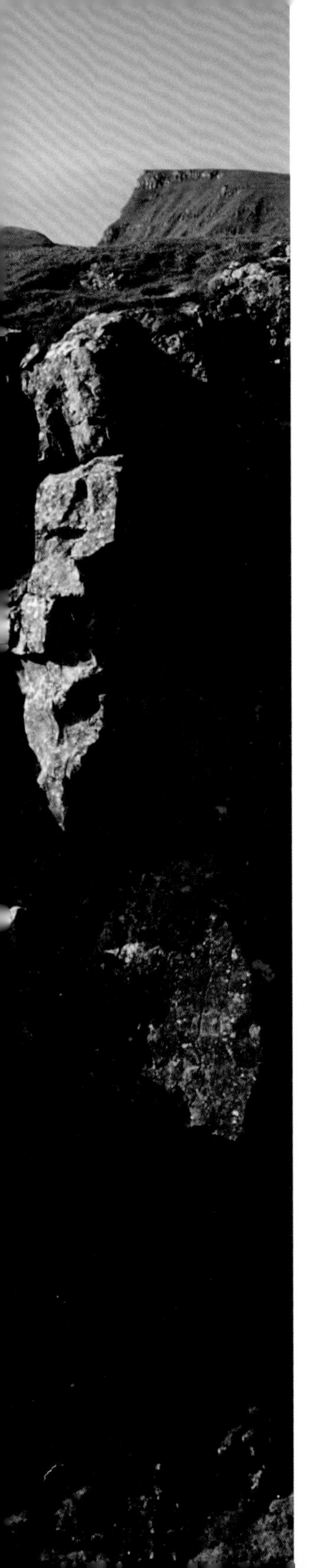

Introduction

We sat above the agitated waters of the Minch at the very northern tip of the Isle of Skye. Beyond the shoreline were the small islands of Fladda-chuain and Eilean Trodday and beyond those rocky outposts, seen in dim outline against the horizon, lay Scalpay and the hills of Harris.

We had come to Rubha Hunish, one of the wildest and loneliest corners of Skye, in the hope of witnessing a flaming red, orange and golden sunset for which the Western Isles are renowned. But dark clouds had rolled across the sky, violent rain showers sporadically swept in from the sea and battered this rugged peninsula whose wind-ruffled moorland culminates in impressively steep basalt cliffs. The rock climbers in our team gazed at them longingly. But we weren't at Rubha Hunish to climb rock. This was the start of a television walk for BBC Scotland that would take me through the Isle of Skye, a journey on foot that would link two of the most impressive landscapes in Scotland – the Trotternish ridge and the Cuillin.

I knew Skye reasonably well. Numerous sorties to the Cuillin had become pilgrimages over the years – where else in the UK can one pay homage to the Norse/Celtic mountain gods? And I had tramped the length of the Trotternish ridge some 30 years ago, but it's only in recent years that I began peeking around the corners of these two landscapes, peering over the horizons of the pinnacled ridges so see what lay beyond. I had become intrigued by my new discoveries, enthralled by the history and the wildlife and the geology and the Celtic heritage of this island that once upon a time, in the Mesolithic period, would have been a very desirable location to live, a wooded place of richness, with a Mediterranean climate, seas full of fish and forests full of animals.

Looking south down the Trotternish Ridge

Camp at Rubha Hunish

But volcanic activity and the scourings and gougings of the glaciers had changed the face of the land. Just as the two major landscapes were linked geologically, the time had come, I decided, to link them together into a long walk.

Everyone knows about the Skye Cuillin. The savage grandeur of these Alpine-looking mountains is world famous and Munro-baggers know that these will be the most technical hills they will have to climb. Indeed, the vast majority of Munro-baggers now hire a guide to traverse the peaks and pinnacles of the Cuillin, an adventure that reaches a thrilling climax on the slim wedge of gabbro that's known as the Inaccessible Pinnacle. But immediately to the south of us lay a rolling escarpment of basalt, the "best high level promenade in Scotland" as it was described by Sheriff Alexander Nicolson away back in the nineteenth century. These are the hills of Trotternish, the green hills that look to the tumbled landscapes of mainland Scotland.

We intended to spend the night here at the tip of the ridge's northern finger, a wild and remote camp on a grassy headland, with the expanse of sea on three sides. But after eating supper, before we crept into our tents for the night, we took a short stroll to a rocky headland and gazed out to sea for a time – we had been told this was a prime spot for watching Minke whales. I tend to take these suggestions with a pinch of salt – I rarely have such wildlife spotting luck, but within minutes of settling down someone yelled "Thar she blows", or words to that effect, and sure enough, about a hundred metres offshore, slicing though the gurgling, grueing sea surface, we saw the arched shape and fin of one of these incredible sea mammals. It may not have been watching Humpback whales off Vancouver Island or kayaking with Orcas off the coast of Alaska but watching Minke whales from one of a number of coastal vantage points in the UK can add a thrilling moment or two to any coastal walk. Indeed, a whole new whale and dolphin-spotting industry appears to be encouraging many folk out to sea to spot these phenomenal beasts for themselves, armed not with harpoons, as in former years, but with cameras.

The Common Minke whale is a fascinating animal and can be categorized into two or three subspecies – the North Atlantic, the North Pacific and the Dwarf Minke whale. All Minkes are part of the marine family that includes the Humpback whale, the Fin whale, Bryde's whale and the fabled Blue whale. Common Minke whales (the kind you are likely to see from our coasts) are distinguished from other whales by a white band on each flipper. The body is usually black or dark-grey above and white underneath. Most of the length of the back, including the dorsal fin and blowholes, appears at once when the whale surfaces to breathe. The whale then breathes several times at short intervals before 'deep-diving' for anything between two and 20 minutes. Deep dives are preceded by a pronounced arching of the back, and this is what we saw from our vantage point on Rubha Hunish.

The larger whales typically leap about three-quarters out of the water. They then twist on their axis prior to re-entry which is believed to protect their internal organs from the shock of their huge bodies hitting the water. Minkes can swim close to shore and often enter bays, inlets and estuaries, and throughout the country whale- and dolphin-spotting has been an integral part of the new eco-tourism economy. Popular Minke whale viewing areas include the Isle of Man, County Cork in Ireland and the Islands of Mull and Skye.

Rubha Hunish

It's often difficult to distinguish one Minke whale from another and in most cases they either travel singly or congregate in small pods of about 2-3 whales. It was hard to say how many we saw – there were about 20 appearances but whether that was all the same whale or a small pod I have no idea.

It's often been said that the largest wild mammal we can see in the UK is the red deer stag, but an adult Minke whale is considerably bigger than that. Minke whales can grow to about 25-30 feet (8-9 m) long, and weigh about 6-7.5 tons (5.4-6.8 tonnes). Females are about 2 feet (0.6 m) longer than males, as with all baleen whales. The largest Minke whale recorded was about 35 feet (10.5 m) long weighing 9.5 tons. Minke whales have not been the target of whalers since a world-wide moratorium on whaling in the late 1980s, but Japan, Iceland and Norway have continued hunting for Minkes on so-called 'scientific' grounds. These 'scientific grounds' have been roundly criticized by many environmental organisations and it's well known that these countries tend to have ambitions towards resuming large scale whaling operations. But how did the Minke whale get its name? One tale suggests that a German whaler by the name of Meineke mistook one of these small whales for a blue whale – to the amusement of his fellow whalers. From then on whalers called them 'Meineke's whale', which eventually became Minke or mink.

Despite the weather, and our disappointment at not being able to begin our television walk from the spectacle of a western sunset, we walked back to our tents in a state of mild euphoria, that condition of heightened awareness we reach when we are fortunate enough to encounter animals that are truly wild. Here we were, a hard-bitten, seen-it-all television crew, five grown men all experienced in the ways and sights of the outdoors, yet we were as thrilled as children, as excited as puppies.

Not for the first time, I lay in my tent and pondered on this curious reaction to seeing nature in the raw. It seems that we are so removed nowadays from the sights and sounds of nature that any close encounter with wildlife gets us really excited. In watching a whale arching into its dive, or wondering at the majestic flight of an eagle it would appear that we become aware of the simple magic of the moment, an instinctive recognition of the existence of order, a determined pattern behind the behaviour of things, a celebration of order and harmony, and that can be both exciting and curiously comforting. Over the years I've been blessed with several face-to face encounters with wild animals – bears, wolves, coyotes and here at home smaller but no less exciting species like otters and badgers. All of them have given me a sense of beauty and magic, sensations that never fail to fill me with hope and optimism, feelings that can be curiously rare in a sometimes dreary world.

I think we all slipped into our sleeping bags that night with a renewed awareness that even in the gathering dusk we had witnessed something of rare beauty, all the more astonishing because the sighting was so unexpected, as was its effect on us. But this is far from a contemporary phenomenon. Ancient Celtic spirituality was based on a deep connection with the natural world, and the Celts had an intellectual curiosity about all the creatures they shared their lives with. Perhaps our sighting of the Minke whale stirred some ancient memory of Manannan mac Llyr, the sea god, the northern equivalent of the Greek deity Poseidon?

At the start of the trail

Winter at Storr rocks

And where better to learn more about the lives of the Celtic people and their nature-based beliefs than here on Skye? On this long walk through the island, the *Skitis* of the Celts, I hoped to understand something more of the people who inhabited the island in years gone by. Indeed, about 8,000 years ago, the island that we now know as Skye was home to a well ordered and organised community, living from the fruits and berries of the abundant woodlands and forest, enjoying the best of the sea's harvest and in a climate that was considerably warmer and drier than Skye's climate is today. The Celts came here much later, from Ireland, and sensed the presence of their gods in every nook and cranny, on every hill and crag, in every corrie and loch. Landscape and weather and an affinity with wild nature made up the very fabric of their lives.

In our modern world it's very easy to lose this connection with wild nature; indeed it's very easy to lose the source of creativity in ourselves. Twenty-first century living and the economic and social pressure it brings can easily make us contract and become fearful, but the Celts believed in an Otherworld, a realm of the imagination where your mind could expand and flow, circle and explore. This realm of the mind could be entered by anyone who knew the entrance, the portal to this world of dreams, and the Celtic people continuously watched out for signs that an entrance to the Otherworld was at hand. One of these portals was through the eyes of a wild animal, an animal that would look at you and invite you to follow it... Perhaps some enduring connection still haunts us through the sightings of wild animals, perhaps this euphoria that we felt as we trekked back to our tents on Rubha Hunish was a link to the subtle, evanescent place that our ancestors cherished as a realm of treasure and inspiration. Little did I know at that early point in our walk through Skye that in the days to come I was to experience this sense of delight with the natural world over and over again. Little did I realize how much of that ancient Celtic spirit still flows around the hills and glens of this fabulous island.

In over 40 years of wandering through the wild places of Scotland I've often tried to define the curiously quintessential element that gives these mountains, coastlines and forests their essential character and vibrancy. It's an element I've never experienced anywhere else in the world. Heritage is too weak a word for it, too bland. It's more mystical than that, perhaps some kind of indwelling spirit born of Celtic ancestry, a kind of spirit-of-place that draws visitors to this uncompromising land teetering on the very edge of Europe where we can wander in peace and take time to wonder at its grandeur. We can even experience the resonances of the land's turbulent past. It's undoubtedly a place that can bring tears to nostalgic eyes and, at the same time, music to the lips. But what creates such a land? Is it the people, or the landscape features, or the weather and its atmospheres? Or is it a combination of all these things, the intertwining of cultures and history, life and death, with the ever changing landscapes of mountain and sea? Indeed, what happens to this land when you remove the people from it?

Crags at Rubha Hunish

Let me tell you. You are left with a wilderness-of-sorts, a man-made wilderness perhaps but one laced with the whiffs and taints of days gone by. In these highlands and islands landscapes you can never shrug aside the ghosts of yesterday. You can't ignore the ancient shielings and the dry stone walls; the skeletal outlines of the run-rigs and the lazybeds and the stark silhouettes of the gable walls still standing. You can't dismiss the souterains and the stone circles, or the ancient brochs and duns. From so many areas of the highlands and islands of Scotland the people have gone but their memories remain. As do the hills, the forests, the lochs and most impressively, the rock.

Consider that rock. Much of it has seen the passage of history from maybe twenty, thirty, some say sixty million years. The rocks were higher then and extended west beyond the now blunted teeth of St Kilda – before the scouring of water, then ice, carved this great tableland into mountainous shapes; many hundreds of them. Consider too the indented and convoluted western seaboard of Scotland, a mere 320km (200 miles) as the sea-eagle flies but well over ten times that when you follow the crazy contortions of its incredibly varied coastline. Or think of the remnants of the ancient Caledonian pinewoods of Perthshire, Speyside and Deeside, memorials to the once-massive forest that covered much of this country. The islands too – the Hebrides, Shetland and Orkney – are all rich in beauty and variety without equal. The Isle of Skye is possibly the most famous of them all and the finest way to explore it, indeed the only way to explore it, is on foot. Folk have been climbing and walking on Skye since history began. The roads are new, laid down less than 200 years ago and before they appeared everyone used tracks, or simply took to the heather. This tradition of *de facto* freedom to roam in the wild places of Scotland is jealously guarded and new legislation has simply changed that *de facto* right to a *de jure* one – everyone now has the legal right to walk the hills and wild places of Scotland as they wish, provided they act responsibly.

And what rich rewards are there to be discovered in this land of the mountain and the flood, this wild land that forms a part of the rough bounds of Europe.

Looking south from the Cuillin ridge

Whether it be climbing the soaring mountains, hiking long distance treks down the peninsulas or through the glens or taking coastline rambles, Skye's spirit-of-place will infuse your own spirit and draw you back time and time again, just as it does mine. Indeed, I like to equate my own relationship with Skye with that of the endless knot of the ancient Celts. These people had a fascination with this symbolic knot – an elaborately interlaced line that had no beginning or end. The endless knot has been described by scholars as a kind of Celtic mandala, a cosmic mind-map, expressing the Celtic belief in eternity – a transcendental state beyond the material world. For me it represents the various journeys that I've enjoyed on Skye over the best part of 40 years, the regularity of the visits, the awareness that the end of a particular journey is never the absolute end, that I will return and start the relationship all over again. It's an ongoing process, a process in which I continually learn more and more about this fascinating island and, as I learn more about it, the desire to return as often as possible grows stronger. Each visit, each journey, is merely another curve on the endless knot of time.

Part of this Skye addiction is the sense of Celtic history that remains here. Only recently a friend wrote to me to tell me about a new house he was building – an eco house with a green oak frame, oak cladding, sheepswool insulation, turbine in the burn etc – on the west coast of Scotland. He was particularly enthralled with the situation of his new house and the view from it, over to Eigg and the Rum Cuillin and beyond to Skye – and how the weather, light and perspective played on and between the islands. He went on to suggest there was something about the geometry that draws you in. "When the sun sets behind the conical peak of Trolleval it's hard not to get all poetic," he said. But he did. He went on to say that he'd been watching a television documentary about one of ancient Egypt's Pharaohs, Akhenaten, and how he rebuilt his capital at Amarna specifically because the setting sun made poetic geometry with a conical mountain. Could the ancient Celts have held similar views, he asked? I guess they might have done. Certainly the ancient Celtic people looked to the west as their eternal resting place, probably because the sun rises in the east and dies in the west. Over the distant western horizon lay Tir nan Og, the mystical land of the ever-young.

On a broader theme the Celts tended to build their temples or cells sited in such a way as to exploit the energies of the earth. A shrine to Manannan, the lord of the waters, might be built near a river. Certain places held certain kinds of power, depending on factors such as the stone underlying them, the kinds of vegetation that grew and the positioning of nearby hills or waterways. Some places were for healing, some for energizing, some were conducive to contemplation while others may have had an uncomfortable or uncanny atmosphere. Certainly, the ancient Celts knew few cities or towns, and their landscapes were generally those of forests, woods, mountains or seashores. The natural world was vitally important to them – spiritually so, for the sky and the unspoiled land provided a relationship between man and the cosmos, a relationship that is almost unknown to us today, a relationship – not unknown to other ancient belief systems – that our modern society, in its over-reliance on materialism, has allowed to wither and atrophy. I find it fascinating that the Celts recognized nature as a divine mirror of the cycles and power of the universe and saw animals, lakes, trees, stones, the sun, moon, and seasons as reflections of a sovereign God. It's not surprising then, that the early Christians missionaries were attracted by Celtic beliefs and the early religions were often intermingled.

My friend's thoughts about the ancient Egyptians were probably on the right lines – such ancient belief systems appear to be almost universal, which probably indicates that these early people traveled widely, but my own interest stems from the fact that so many of these early belief systems held the land in much more reverence that we do today. There's little doubt in my mind that while we enjoy all the materialistic and scientific benefits of the twenty-first century, we have lost something much more essential – that awareness of the vital importance of the natural world, a reverence for the land. It's perhaps fair to say that our ancestors relied on the land more than we do but something inside me can't help thinking we have lost something much more important than mere possessions.

In the *Book of Llanrwst*, author Nigel Pennick compares features of the landscape as reflections of corresponding human parts: "The first is the earth, which is inert and heavy, and from it proceeds the flesh; the second are the stones, which are hard, and the substance of bones; the third is water, which is moist and cold, and is the substance of the blood; the fourth is salt, which is briny and sharp, and from it are the nerves, and the temperament of feelings, as regards bodily sense and faculty; the fifth is the firmament or wind, out of which proceeds the breathing; the sixth is the sun, which is clear and fair, and from it proceed the fire, or bodily heat, the light and colour; the seventh is the Holy Ghost, from whom issues the soul and life; and eighth is Christ, that is, the intellect, wisdom and the light of soul and life."

I find it intriguing that Nigel Pennick's comparisons almost mirror the words of lightweight backpacking guru Ray Jardine. I made a television programme with Ray in Oregon a number of years ago and not only did I learn a huge amount about wilderness backpacking from him, I also learned much about how we can build a stronger relationship with the land. Incidentally, Ray's sources are not of the ancient Celts, but of the native North Americans. In an email message after our trip through the Three Sisters Wilderness in Oregon Ray wrote: "We might remember that despite our overwhelming technology we are still flesh and bone. Our bodies are an integral part of Mother Earth. The air we breathe is her breath, rippling the grasses in the meadow. The water we drink is her life-blood, tumbling from the snowy heights. Our flesh comes from the soft, rich earth, our bone from the sun-baked rocks. Every molecule in us is not our own, but a part of Mother Earth. We are borrowing that molecule from her, and will have to give it back when we leave."

Winter Cuillin fron Glen Sligachan

Other belief systems from throughout the world share that reverence, that intimacy with the natural world. I've had similar conversations with the Bedouin in the deserts of Wadi Rum; with the Berbers of the High Atlas in Morocco, with the Sherpas of Nepal and most notably, with native people of Australia. Perhaps as backpackers, as people who walk through the land and take spiritual sustenance from the land, we can learn something from those Celtic people who lived here before us, lessons that we can take home with us and help to re-shape our lives in these environmentally-challenged times. Lessons, perhaps that we can teach others?

Earlier in the year, my wife Gina and I had enjoyed a most amazing reconnaissance trip to Skye, from Duntulm in the north of Trotternish to Elgol, the coastal hamlet that offers some of the most magnificent views across the sea waters of Loch Scavaig towards the Cuillin. Our plan, like the best, was simple. In astonishingly fine weather we walked from Duntulm down the length of the Trotternish ridge all the way to Portree, visiting the two volcanic wonders of Trotternish, The Quiraing and The Storr, en route. From Portree we wandered down a quiet and tranquil road past Braes, scene of the last battle in Britain, before following a coast path along the west shore of Loch Sligachan to the famous hotel of the same name (some claim it as the cradle of Scottish mountaineering). From there the footpath down Glen Sligachan took us below the skirts of both Red and Black Cuillin to the high pass over to Scotland's finest loch, Coruisk, before a skirmish with the infamous Bad Step and the scenic coastal path to Camusunary and Elgol.

Elgol peninsula from Sgurr na Stri

Old ruins at Boreraig

With a television crew – my old friend and colleague Richard Else, cameraman Dominic Scott and safety officer Paul Tattersall – I repeated the route again, but this time we continued past Camasunary, over Bla Bheinn and down to Torrin and the old crofters trail to the deserted villages of Suisnish and Boreraig. Beyond Boreraig the line of an old narrow-gauge railway took us past the former marble mines of Ben Suardal all the way to Broadford on the coast.

This so-called Skye Trail, for want of a better title, is not an original route; it's not a backpacking journey that we've thought up by studying maps, completing reconnaissance visits and consulting with locals. It is, if anything, a straightforward and logical route that takes in some of the finest features of Skye and for me, connects the two finest landscapes on the island, that of the Trotternish ridge and the Cuillin. A number of years ago a friend of mine, the photographer David Paterson, wrote a superb book called *A Long Walk Through Skye*. He began his route at Armadale, close to the southern tip of Skye's Sleat Peninsula, and walked north to Duntulm Castle, a journey of some 120km (77 miles). While I greatly admire David's persistence in walking up the rough and often difficult trackless coasts of Sleat and Loch Eishort, I was keen to stay on paths or tracks almost all the way. Having said that, I'm well aware that the paths and tracks on the Trotternish ridge are merely the faint trods of other walkers, but at least there is a twenty-odd mile rocky escarpment to follow!

Sunrise over the hills of the mainland

For some time I've felt that the handful of 'official' long distance trails we have in Scotland are not entirely satisfactory. Of them all, only the West Highland Way has been really successful – indeed many would claim it's being loved to death and part of the reason of its overwhelming popularity is the absence of attractive alternatives. The Southern Upland Way, between Portpatrick and Cockburnspath in the Borders, was the UK's first 'official' coast to coast trail but at 340km (220 miles) it's too long for most people who can usually only afford a two-week holiday at the most. That route also tends to miss out the main centres of population, and surely one of the main reasons for a long distance trail is to help the economies of some of the small towns or villages it passes through?

"You are left with a wilderness-of-sorts, a man-made wilderness perhaps but one laced with the whiffs and taints of days gone by. In these highlands and islands landscapes you can never shrug aside the ghosts of yesterday… From so many areas of the highlands and islands of Scotland the people have gone but their memories remain. As do the hills, the forests, the lochs and most impressively, the rock."

Neither the Speyside Way nor the Great Glen Way are particularly attractive routes. The first fails to run the full length of the Spey, Scotland's fastest flowing river, and misses out the stretch between the source and the village of Newtonmore, certainly the most attractive stretch between source and sea. The Great Glen Way runs through commercial forestry plantations for much of its course, but has nevertheless become popular amongst mountain bikers who enjoy riding along the broad forest tracks. A number of years ago a good friend and colleague of mine, Roger Smith, helped to devise an excellent route in the Borders between Melrose and Lindisfarne. It's called the St Cuthbert's Way, and although it does not have the status of a 'national trail' it has nevertheless become very popular. Another 'unofficial' route is the Cape Wrath Trail between Fort William and the most north-westerly part of the Scottish mainland, a route that really only exists on a website.

Two years ago Richard Else and I made a television programme about a route through the old county of Sutherland. We called it The Sutherland Trail and in 2009 we published the first guidebook to it. It's our hope that the route will be 'adopted' by the communities it passes through, communities who might benefit from the increased trade such a route brings. We hope the Skye Trail might do the same. Already a very popular website for hillwalkers, www.walkhighlands.co.uk, has created a page dedicated to The Skye Trail and the operators of the website have indicated they will work with marketing organizations on Skye to try and make the route better known. It's no less than the Isle of Skye, and the route itself, deserves. It is a spectacular walk and I recommend it to you with a passion…

TROTTERNISH

Map
Ordnance Survey 1:50,000 Landranger Sheet 23 (North Skye).

Distance
45 kilometres/27 miles.

Approx. time
2-3 days.

Terrain
Rough footpaths to Duntulm then a short section of road before open moorland. That's followed by undulating hill country, mostly pathless. Short road section at end of the ridge into Portree.

Trail Information

Route

Leave Rubha Hunish and climb on to the Meall Tuath escarpment. Now follow rough footpaths S to Duntulm. Follow A855 E to Kilmaluag and take minor road S to Connista. Follow Kilmaluag River then Lon Horro S and SE into Coire Mhic Eachainn. Climb steep slopes to Sron Vourlinn ridge. Follow ridge S for a short distance then drop down steeply to the W to follow a footpath below the cliffs S to below The Prison. Turn right and ascend steep scree slopes to visit The Quiraing. Return to footpath and follow it SW to meet the Staffin to Uig road. Cross the road and climb the slopes of Bioda Buidhe. Follow the escarpment edge S over Beinn Edra, Sgurr a'Mhadaidh Ruaidh, The Storr and Ben Dearg. Continue S on the ridge over A'Chorra-bheinn and Creag an Fhithich to meet the A855 road at Dun Gerashader. Follow the road S into Portree.

Accommodation

Duntulm Castle Hotel, Duntulm, Trotternish, Isle of Skye, IV51 9UF
01470 552213
www.duntulmcastle.co.uk

Fairly basic accommodation, standard pub food but tremendous location. The nearest accommodation to the start of the walk at Rubha Hunish.

Public Transport

Bus services on the Isle of Skye are excellent. Check out the times at www.stagecoachbus.com. There is a free long-stay car park in Portree and you can catch a bus to Duntulm from the main square in Portree. At the end of the Skye Trail there are regular buses from Broadford to Portree.

Traveline: 0871 200 2233 or www.travelinescotland.com provides a comprehensive journey planning service.

TROTTERNISH

It was on a June day of blustery winds and rain storms that Harry McShane and I turned our backs on the advancing veils of grey showers that were sweeping across the Minch from the purple hills of Harris, to walk south over the spine of the Trotternish peninsula in Northern Skye. At the time I thought this walk, from the old castle of Duntulm to Portree, the capital of the Isle of Skye, was without equal in the whole of Scotland. A glance at the Ordnance Survey map of northern Skye will show you the great feature of Trotternish – a long and winding escarpment of basalt cliffs running in a southerly direction from the steep peaks of Sgurr Mhor and Sron Vourlinn near Duntulm, to the bare moorland above Portree. That outing, some thirty years ago, was my first introduction to walking on Skye outside the Cuillin and I knew little about the geology of the area, virtually nothing about the immense expanse of time and power and energy that had created such a magnificent natural feature.

The sheer east-facing cliffs of this great ridge are sills, or sheets of lava, immensely thick, intruded between the upper and lower layers of the basalt plateaux, after they were laid down. The upper basalt sheets have been cut back to the ridge and have left the long intrusive sills in a long line from Portree up the length of the peninsula and out to sea as far north as the Shiant Isles. While the east-facing cliffs are sheer, the western slopes of the ridge are in complete contrast. Long and gentle grassy slopes run all the way up to the rim of the cliffs, the turf shorn short and smooth by the continual grazing of sheep and rabbits and by the constant caress, and occasional battering, of the western breezes.

The iconic view of the Storr rocks

Approaching the Trotternish ridge from Kilmaluag

The summits of the ridge are not particularly high, reaching 719m/2358ft above sea level at the trig point on The Storr, but on a clear day these lowly hills offer superb panoramas from as far west as St Kilda, beyond the Outer Isles, over the jagged outline of Skye's chief attraction, the Cuillin, to the great mountain massifs of Torridon, Gairloch and Applecross on the mainland.

These hills may lack the excitement of the Cuillin verticalities, and by no stretch of the imagination can you experience the lonely isolation of a Knoydart or Fisherfield landscape, but the easy and undulating walking, in continual view of the sea on both sides, has a charm of its own. The salt air is vibrant and heady, the short turf makes the physical act of walking a real joy and the tiny dots of the whitewashed cottages and the tracing of green fields on the moors below add a strong sense of human interest to the beauty of nature.

In springtime and early summer a profusion of wild flowers decorates the predominant greenery with the extremely rare *Koenigia islandica* – Iceland purslane – growing on some of the summits. You are also in the constant company of birds, from wheatears, dippers, snipe, pipits, plovers and gulls to eagles, both golden eagles and sea eagles. But the real delights of Trotternish are neither pastoral or gentle. At the north end of the peninsula, opposite Staffin Bay, the wild towers and crazy pinnacles which form the battlements of The Quiraing, a collapsed lava slip, present an intriguing and eerie prospect, while further south, below the frowning cliffs of The Storr, another slip has culminated in the weird formations of the Old Man of Storr and his shorter neighbours, eroded basaltic columns that throw their great spires skyward in a jumble of ghostly pinnacles.

Following our wild camp at Rubha Hunish we backtracked south along muddy sheep tracks to Duntulm Bay and the remains of its once noble castle. The weather had deteriorated during the night and boisterous winds toyed with us as we tried to film the castle, set on its rocky promontory. Although Dominic, our cameraman, was having some difficulty coping with the ever-changing light I was quite happy with the conditions for there are few places in Scotland as exciting, on a day of crashing surf and billowing storm cloud, as Duntulm Castle. Clinging to its rocky headland that rises sheer from the restless waters of the Minch, the grey ruins show a brave face to the wrath of the north-westerly gales. Despite its exposed position on the north-western tip of the peninsula, the castle, the ancient stronghold of the MacDonalds of the Isles, was a base from which the Lords of the Isles could taunt their enemies and, summoning their forces, sally forth on their war galleys (called 'birlinns') to do battle by sea and defend their sovereignty against the rival kings of Scotland. Duntulm Castle's exposure was its strength.

Ged tha th'n diugh'a d'aibheas fhuar,

Bha thu uair 'a d'aros righ

Though thou art today a ruin cold,

Thou wert once the dwelling of a king.

Duntulm was certainly a "ruin cold" today, as the winds scurried off the sea and discouraged any temptation to linger.

Duntulm Castle

In between grey showers, a strong sun burst from the fast-moving clouds, dazzling off the green waters, and intensifying the colours of the pebbled bays and the distant hues of the hills of Harris. To be honest there isn't much left of the castle today despite its former glory, and if you do try to use your imagination to rustle up some notion of what it might have been like, the warning signs and barriers erected by Historic Scotland bring you back to our health and safety obsessed reality. Essentially the signs warn you to Keep Out. With some judicious camera positions we managed to avoid the wooden fences and signs and I tried to evoke some of the atmosphere of Viking times and later, in the fifteenth century, when the castle was in its prime.

Tradition would suggest that Duntulm Castle was built on the site of an earlier Viking stronghold, the Dun of David, and it's claimed even today, most probably erroneously, that a long indentation on the rocks below the castle walls was made by the keels of Viking galleys. Norse influence was very much felt here on Skye so it's entirely possible that this site was used by Vikings but we definitely know that, according to Skene's Celtic Scotland, published in 1580, "Thair was an castell in Troutrnes callit Duncolmen quhairof the wallis standis yet." It was later, the early part of the eighteenth century, that Sir Donald Gorm, chief of the MacDonalds of the Isles, made use of those still-standing walls and resurrected a fortress on the cliffs above Tulm Bay but his stay at his new castle didn't last long. Following the Battle of Killiecrankie and the failure of the first Jacobite Rising in 1715 he returned to Duntulm to die, a broken man. As a Jacobite supporter his estates were later forfeited by the Crown, and it's most likely that during this period of forfeiture Duntulm Castle fell into ruin. The new chief, Sir Alexander MacDonald, took stones from Duntulm to build his new home at Monkstadt in Sleat and later still, in the nineteenth century, the farmer at Duntulm blew up the remaining structures – to get stone for a wall he wanted to build!

Written like that, I guess the factual history of Duntulm Castle is boringly prosaic, with little appeal, but tradition has a fine way of interweaving tales and legends with what we believe as truth, and we end up with something much more alluring and charismatic. Legend would have it that Donald Gorm, who was apparently something of the black sheep of the family, died in Edinburgh but came back in spirit form to haunt Duntulm Castle, forcing the family to abandon it to the winds and the sea spray. Another tale suggests that a nurse somehow managed to drop the infant heir to the clan chief out of a window in the castle from where the child fell to his death on the rocks below. For her clumsiness the nurse was tied and cast adrift in a boat full of holes. It's been said her cries and sobs can still be heard on stormy nights… The family, shattered by the tragedy, left the castle, unable to remain in a place with such dreadful associations.

The nurse's window at Duntulm

Curiously, a similar incident forced the MacLeods, traditional enemies of the MacDonalds, to leave their castle at Glenelg. Clumsy nurses appear to have been fashionable in the eighteenth century.

From the ruins of the castle, we followed the scenic road east for a couple of miles through the scattered crofts of Kilmaluag to where a minor road turned off due south to a croft marked on the OS map as Connista. Low-lying cottages made an attractive foreground to the bare moorland, backed by the looming cliffs of Sgurr Mhor and Sron Vourlinn. The prominent nose of Vourlinn was our first objective, the beginnings of the long series of cliff edges that would guide us all the way to Portree. Sron Vourlinn is known locally as Sron Bhiornal, after a Norse princess who once lived on the island. Before she died, she requested that she might be buried high on the hill so that her tomb might look across the sea and across Scotland to her native Norway. There is nothing there to mark her grave but it's claimed she was laid to rest on a grassy ledge on the cliff, about 20 metres below the crest of the hill.

At the start of the Trotternish ridge

Appoaching The Quiraing with Staffin beyond

It's about a kilometre across the moor from Connista to Coire Mhic Eachainn, which separates Vourlinn from bulky Sgurr Mhor. A signpost, marked 'Footpath to The Quiraing' cheered me up immensely, as I remembered the route to be something of a wet bog-trot. In fact the 'footpath' didn't last very long. It took us down to a new wooden bridge over the Kilmaluag River before vanishing in a turmoil of heather knolls. The climb wasn't too difficult, and we followed the line of the Lon Horro burn over the moors, with several patches of peat bog to negotiate, but our attention was constantly held by the harsh crying of snipe, protesting the disturbance we caused, the bustle of dippers on the fast-flowing stream and the constant outpouring of joy that is the song of the skylark. Gradually the slope became steeper and steeper and we passed from bog-cotton strewn wetlands to the springy cropped turf of the hill.

Looking out from The Quiraing

In a short time we stood at the crumbling edge of the precipice; one moment easy-angled slope, the next moment a void! This is the great feature of the Trotternish ridge, the dramatic contrast between bare and featureless moorland and these great cliffs, often overhanging and always high.

This is a good spot to stop and take in the surroundings. By now the glowering clouds had been swept away by the breeze and the sun was trying hard to light up the scene before us. A footpath dropped down into a shallow valley below, a valley glinting with sparkling lochans and prickled with jagged volcanic upthrusts. Away behind us, in the green waters of the Minch, the island of Trodday lay close to the shore; beyond it was the outline of the distant Shiant Isles, and even further away, the sun was just catching the horizon hills of Harris. The peaks on the Scottish mainland were visible only as a dark mass – haze made them barely discernable, but in front of us, southwards, the progression of the steep noses of the escarpment flowed on like the crests of giant waves, towering to the sky, and fading into the haze beyond the notable outline of The Storr.

From Vourlinn a crumbling cliff edge runs south to eventually reach the summit slopes of Meall na Suiramach, 543m/1781ft, the hill that is usually, erroneously, called The Quiraing. The Quiraing (a fold, or pen) is in fact the name of a collection of spires, rocks and volcanic debris that has been split away from the rock face, and since we were keen to visit this curious amphitheatre, we agreed that the sensible thing to do was to drop down below the level of the escarpment and enter The Quiraing from below. A slanting grassy shelf led us down through the cliffs and we soon reached the floor of the hidden valley that runs the length of the escarpment. Sheltered now from the wind we wandered through a wood of weird spires and pinnacles, the remnants of a volcanic age, with the great black cliff to our right sombre and dripping wet with running water. Only in volcanic Iceland have I seen formations like those below The Quiraing; contorted, bent and strangely malevolent, like crooked fingers of rock beckoning you towards some otherworld. The mystic quality of the place is further accentuated by the lavish lushness of the slope; wild flowers grow in abundance, and the grass is an intense shade of green, which seems to soften the harshness of the landscape almost to the point of surrealism.

A good footpath follows the base of the cliff south and we followed this past two small reed fringed lochs, Loch Hasco and Loch Fada. A short distance later, below a huge prow of basalt known as The Prison, we saw how the great cliff had become riven by deep gullies and enormous splits. Here was the route into the inner recesses of the hidden stronghold of The Quiraing. We left our packs by the path and, unencumbered, scrambled up the loose scree slopes and into the shadows of this bewildering jumble of precipices, pinnacles and hollows. Above us immense crags, blocks and spires loomed high, scree slopes led us up through narrow fissures into a giant amphitheatre. Great slices of rock, weathered and cracked, stood apart from the main cliff and through these fissures we could gaze out to the contrasting pastoral scene below; the tiny whitewashed crofts shrunken to insignificance, the green fields, rolling and soft, and the distant swell of the sea breaking its surf on the great curve of Staffin Bay.

Another surprise awaited us. In this world of Titan verticalities of grey and black upthrusts, it seems almost unreal to come across a high rounded table of cropped lush grass, as flat and smooth as a bowling green, so surely one would think, the work of some supernatural force.

The Table

This is The Table, the jewel of The Quiraing. A slanting ledge runs onto the surface of this broad upthrust and behind it, perhaps in sympathy with the lushness of the unexpected turf, the dripping wet cliff face is a veritable rock garden. Yellow globe-flowers, red and white campion, blue butterwort and sprays of golden roseroot offer a splash of colour to the glistening black rock – the Hanging Gardens of Babylon couldn't have been any finer. Almost exaggerating the splendour of the place, a heavy silence hung around us. No wind breathed in here, no rustling of grass, no crashing streams; only the sound of our footsteps and the exclamations of our delight broke the cathedral hush. This, we decided, could well have been the setting for Tolkien's Rivendell, home to Elrond and his elvin folk. What a place to spend a contemplative weekend! As we prepared to film on The Table I tried to remember the details of a local tale, which recalls an annual shinty match that used to be played here. I couldn't remember if it was held every Midsummer's Day, or every New Year's Day.

Eventually logic held sway and I realised that virtually every single shinty player that I know would be physically incapable of playing the game on New Year's Day. It must have been a Midsummer Day match!

We eventually dragged ourselves away from The Table, down dark corridors of scree, past the highest of all the pinnacles, the towering spire of The Needle, 40 metres in height, tapering at both the top and bottom. More slopes of black scree slid us down to the footpath in front of The Prison, the southerly outpost of The Quiraing, a massive assemblage of rock like some ancient fortress. No-one appears to know how this rock got its name, but it's claimed the ghost of an ancient cleric used to emerge from the rock from time to time until eventually his spirit was exorcised by some good and saintly person. We followed the path back to where our packs lay, then set out along a beautifully terraced track which ran along the top of the slope just below the foot of the cliffs. Below us the narrow Staffin to Uig road wound its way up to the escarpment in a series of tight hairpin bends before continuing across to the long smooth slopes running down to Uig Bay. Beyond the road the escarpment nose undulated south as impressively as ever.

The Quiraing's remarkable pinnacles

Away below us, on the moorland, some crofters were busy 'at the peat' digging and cutting the turf into manageable sizes, the long thin strips of their endeavour like little scars on the surface of the moor. We met several other walkers making for The Quiraing from the car park, all of them commenting, with a hint of surprise I suspect, on the quality of the views. On an island where the Cuillin is supposed to be the finest landscape feature, many folk are more than a little surprised that there can be such a contrasting natural feature in the north of the island. For many people, the line of the Trotternish ridge is equally as impressive as the Cuillin. It's just different.

This track to the Staffin/Uig road is a remarkably beautiful one with the wide sweep of the shore providing a parallel to the sweeping fringe of the ridge rising tier upon tier to a height of over 600 metres, to where the long rim cuts into the sky. Even on an overcast day like ours the outlook was one of total grandeur, yet soft; a green softness which reminded me so strongly of the west coast of Clare in Ireland. All that was needed to set the scene was the tinkle of a harp and the melancholy wail of the Uillean pipes. We didn't dally by the roadside and managed to avoid the temptations of good traditional Scottish fare like ostrich and kangaroo burgers from the little van that plies its trade there all summer. Instead we pushed on up the easy slopes of Bioda Buidhe. Below us, in the lee of the cliffs, a profusion of rowan trees grew on ledges in the cliffs, remarkable since trees tend to be pretty rare in Trotternish. Several old hill passes cross this backbone of land, passes which were frequently trodden in days gone by but today echo only to the shouts and whistles of the occasional shepherd. Even walkers are few and far between, most visitors climbing to The Quiraing from their cars before driving south to the do the same at Storr. The Bealach nan Coisichean and the Bealach Uige are two of these old passes. Both are low points on the escarpment, at places where the top of the escarpment can be negotiated through the cliffs.

Below the Bealach Uige, nestling darkly into the rock, lies Loch Corcasgil. One day, it was said, a shepherd and his wife were on the hill, passing the time by trundling large boulders over the cliff edge into the dark waters below (as you do) when there was a great turmoil in the surface of the loch and the poor folk saw a huge black horse emerge from the water and swim to the shore, neighing angrily.

Above The Quiraing

The beast, or *each uisge,* a water horse, looked in fury all round, trying to discover who had the audacity to disturb him in his lair. The shepherd and his wife, immediately recognizing the fearsome steed as the dreaded *each uisge*, a beast with the power to change at will into human form, crouched behind a rock which they had just been about to roll into the loch. With wet and gleaming flanks the water horse stood for a while, looked around him, then with a grunt sprang back into the loch and dived below the black waters. The *each uisge*, or water horse, is a common legend on Skye and a number of lonely lochans are said to harbour such a beast, so much so that as recently as 1870 attempts were made to drag some of the lochs to try and capture one. Derek Cooper, in his excellent gazetteer of the Isle of Skye, reminds cynics that they shouldn't condemn the people of Skye as being simple and superstitious because of their belief in the *each uisge*. After all, a countless amount of money has been spent in trying to discover the monster in Loch Ness!

The Needle seen from The Prison

To the south of the Bealach Uige, a fence runs alongside the rim of cliffs to the summit of Beinn Edra, the second highest point on the ridge at just over 610 metres. As we climbed the long slopes, we entered a cap of cloud so we didn't linger on the summit and our thoughts turned from water horses to finding somewhere to camp. Our original plan of camping high on the ridge was now out of the question – the breeze that had been curiously balmy down below now had a fierce edge to it and would have made a night in a tent uncomfortable, if not impossible. Instead, we had to find a way down through the cliffs below the wall of the escarpment. Two more bumps on the ridge had to be crossed before the steepness and height of the cliff relented enough to allow a descent. A grassy rake, steep but doable, allowed us to slither down to some scree slopes, on which we ran with great bounding leaps, the stones and scree sliding down like a grey avalanche. The corrie floor was sheltered from the worst of the wind but the ground was wet and boggy. With a little searching we eventually found a small islet of dry turf where we put the tents up and cooried down inside. Just as we were brewing our first cup of tea the mist and cloud fell like a heavy curtain and the view out to sea evaporated into a grey shroud. As the night went on the wind became stronger and every so often we could hear it sweep over the clifftop behind us, drop into the corrie, and rattle and shake the tent for a few minutes before it died away with a sigh.

By morning it was less windy and the sun shone from a brilliant blue sky. We packed up our belongings, hoisted our packs on our backs and scampered back up onto the ridge again. We made our way south over the Bealach Chaiplin and on along the undulating ridge. The escarpment continually rose and fell and we followed the cliff edge south towards Sgurr a'Mhadaidh Ruaidh, the hill of the red fox, a name which sounds so much more evocative in its Gaelic pronunciation. Try *skoor a vaattie rooya.* This was the scene of an exciting children's book written by Allan Campbell MacLean a number of years ago, a story of skullduggery and adventure which was successfully televised. A descent of the Bealach Hartaval gave us our first glimpse of the Storr rocks across a vast deep-cut corrie before steep slopes had us in climbing mode again. Many of the place names on Skye, indeed in all the Hebrides and much of the western seaboard, are, like Hartaval, of Norse origin, and it's claimed that much Norse blood still flows in the veins of the Sgiannaichs. Indeed, it wasn't until the Battle of Largs in 1263 that Norse occupation of these islands was brought to an end.

The Old Man of Storr

At 719m/2358ft above sea level, The Storr is the highest point of the traverse, a windswept place with a rather broken-down trig pillar. Long views led to the west, by Loch Snizort and away across Vaternish to the distant outlines of MacLeod's Tables. It was cold and windy on the summit and we hurriedly dropped down into Coire Faoin where we would find some shelter. It was there we had arranged to meet up with John Philips, a botanist and Highland Council's senior ranger. John, originally from Barrhead in Renfrewshire, had become interested in natural history at university and after spending some time on Arran had developed an addiction to islands. When a job opportunity came along on Skye he felt he was coming home. A keen sea kayaker, living and working on Skye offers John the ideal environment to live out his passions.

"Away below us, on the moorland, some crofters were busy 'at the peat' digging and cutting the turf into manageable sizes, the long thin strips of their endeavour like little scars on the surface of the moor."

"The Trotternish ridge is the longest landslip feature in Britain," John told me."It's something like 22 miles (34km) of tumbled rock. This top end of Skye is made up from about 25 blankets of molten rock, solidified on top of each other. The molten rock here welled up out of the ground, rather than from big eruptions. The earth's crust was stretching, cracks appearing, and the molten rock came up through the gaps and solidified. The result is that we now have a very unstable sandwich of basalt here. The Earth's crust has tilted, it's been under ice, many times in the past, and every time the ice comes it wears away a little bit more and the whole lot slips down again. And there's about five different layers, landslip events, The last one was probably about 6,500 years ago."

I asked John what it would have looked like here before that last landslip, say in Mesolithic times, about 8,000 years ago? "Well, people would have been living here," he told me, "but this place would have looked quite different. This great pinnacle of the Old Man of Storr wouldn't have been here for example – it appeared subsequently." I commented that the rock appeared to be loose, and friable. "It is", John agreed, "and it breaks down very readily and that's good for me as a botanist. It creates a very rich soil and there are rare plants here that you won't find in many other places in Britain. The Iceland Purslane must be one of the star attractions here." This tiny plant is found high on the Trotternish ridge and despite the fact that the weather was deteriorating – becoming very cold, wet and windy – I was keen to climb back to the ridge to see if we could find it. The first specimen was apparently discovered here in the mid-1950s, and created something of a stir amongst botanists at the time. "Botanists came flocking here," John said, "and got local people to guide them up onto the hill." From the old trig point on The Storr, John checked a bearing on his compass, then began counting steps, in a rough northerly direction. He knew exactly where to look for his 'star attraction', in fact he almost trod on it!

John Philips

Looking south from The Storr's summit

I'm not sure what I expected but the little orange-leafed, shrivelled plant that clung for life on the bare gravelly slope was just a little bit disappointing. I said so, and immediately wished I hadn't. I could sense the disappointment in John's voice. "It gives me a great amount of satisfaction to come here and know where to find it. It's a wee bit past its best now of course but this is an exceedingly rare plant and there are really only two places in Britain where you'll find it. One is the Ardmeanach peninsula on the Isle of Mull – the other is here on Trotternish. When I was here a few weeks ago it was in flower, and was actually very attractive. If you could imagine flowers made up of three greenish-white sepals which together, form a dimpled triangle. As you can see here, when it's not in flower it can be recognised by its red stems, roundish fleshy leaves, and its very small size." Just before we parted, John to head back down to the road, me to continue my traverse of Trotternish, John surprised me by telling me that the Old Man of Storr had over 20,000 people visiting it in the past year. That's a huge number of visitors, many of whom will climb to the summit of The Storr itself. I couldn't help thinking that this precious little plant, the Iceland Purslane, hanging onto life in such a harsh environment, could well be wiped out not by changing weather conditions, but by the trampling of boots.

Our route now lay to the golden west, then south around the corrie rim to descend the grassy slopes to the Bealach Beag. The remainder of the ridge stretched out before us, the long escarpment abutting the flat face of Ben Dearg. The contrast between the dark bastions and weird summits of The Storr and the landscapes to the south is as acute as that between The Quiraing and the softer croft lands of Staffin. The Storr lochs of Leathan and Fada, both of them well stocked with brown trout, reflect the blue of the sky. The valley lies far below, green and inviting – at its further end lay Portree and the twinkling waters of the bay, backed by the tiered slopes of Ben Tianavaig. To the east is the sea, breaking on the skerries of north Raasay and beyond that, the dim and shadowy outline of the Gairloch hills. Rona, with her broken rocks and Raasay of the purple hills lay between us and the mainland and now and then, as the sun peeped from beyond a cloud, a stray drift of light would shine off the coast of Applecross and the mountains beyond.

Looking north from The Storr

The constantly evolving landscape of The Storr

A narrow sound squeezes its way below Portree beneath Ben Tianavaig, and then turns south towards Broadford where it becomes lost under the shadow of Scalpa. In that direction, the Red Hills and the Cuillin dominate the view – the hills of the next few days. But immediately in front of us a potential problem barred further progress. The ridge wound its way slightly south-west over a series of small bumps before its progress became blocked by the steep corrie of Ben Dearg, whose long ridge runs perpendicular to the main one.

On a previous walk down the Trotternish ridge I had avoided a confrontation with this steep climb by dropping down below the ridge from the Bealach Mor where a terraced sheep track bypassed Ben Dearg and Beinn Mheadhonach beyond, to pick its way through a series of drumlins to the moorland above Portree. This time I was keen to see how difficult it was to get onto Ben Dearg without having to take a long detour west to climb on to its western ridge. We confronted the steep grassy slopes head on. The main difficulty was in leaving the main ridge where it abuts onto the steep north slopes of Ben Dearg.

A narrow sheep trod, only about 15cm wide, runs across a very crumbly scree slope and below it steep screes fell away to a jumble of rocks and boulders. A slip here, or if the narrow path crumbled away, could have very serious consequences. I tip-toed onto the narrow, crumbling ledge, like Agag, treading very delicately. Our relief at getting across safely was rather shortlived though as we now faced a steep climb up the grassy corrie wall. From the summit onwards boggy slopes lead gradually down towards Beinn Mheadhonach and the final top of the ridge, A'Chorra-bheinn. It wasn't long before we could see the houses of Portree, the 'port of the king', so named after a royal visit from King James V in 1540. A short walk on a tarmac road past some modern bungalows eventually took us on to the A855 Portree to Staffin road, just north of the town.

Sheriff Nicolson, the Skye poet, once said: "To ascend Storr and follow the mountain ridge the whole way till you come to The Quiraing is no doubt one of the grandest promenades in Skye, commanding wide views in all directions." Sceptics suggest that he never did it himself, but walkers who do choose to tackle the Trotternish ridge will be amply rewarded for their efforts, there's no doubt about that. It's one of the finest long ridge walks in the whole of Scotland and one of the most memorable sections of the Skye Trail.

Portree to Sligachan

Map
Ordnance Survey 1:50,000 Landranger Sheet 23 (North Skye) and Sheet 32 (South Skye).

Distance
20 kilometres/12 miles.

Approx. time
8-10 hours.

Terrain
Busy trunk road leaving Portree then a stretch of lochside and riverside path. Quiet minor road through The Braes followed by a good lochside path.

Trail Information

Route

Leave Portree by the busy A87, but once past the Aros Centre drop down to the left and follow lochside and riverside paths to the bridge over the Varragill River. Follow the B883 through the villages of Conordan, Lower Ollach, Upper Ollach, The Braes to Peinchorran. From the car park there head W along the N shores of Loch Sligachan. There could be awkward river crossings as you approach Sligachan, especially after heavy rain. Follow footpaths to Sligachan campsite and Sligachan Inn.

Accommodation

The Bosville Hotel: 01478 612846
www.bosvillehotel.co.uk

Rosedale Hotel: 01478 613131
www.rosedalehotelskye.co.uk

Coolin View Guest House: 01478 611280
www.coolinview.co.uk

Cuillin Hills Hotel: 01478 612003
www.cuillinhills-hotel-skye.co.uk

Further Information: www.isleofskyeaccommodation.com/centralskye.htm
Bayfield Backpackers: info@skyehostel.co.uk

Portree Independent Hostel: skyehostel@yahoo.co.uk

Torvaig Camp Site, Staffin Road, Portree: 01478 611849

Portree to Sligachan

On our Skye Trail recce trip, Gina and I were in celebratory mood as we tramped down the road in search of the Torvaig camp site. We had left our car in the free car park in Portree and locked away in the boot we had a change of clothes and some food for the next few days backpacking, the continuation of our journey that would take us down through The Braes, along the shore of Loch Sligachan to the Sligachan Inn then down the length of Glen Sligachan to Coruisk, Camasunary and eventually to Elgol. Not a bad itinerary to look forward to.

But first we had a night in the fleshpots of Skye's biggest settlement. Originally known as Kiltaraglen, the town's name was changed after King James V graced the place with his presence, plus a fleet of warships, away back in 1540. It wasn't a social call – he was apparently visiting the island in an attempt to get the island clans to support him. The King had set sail from the port of Leith, his entourage a dozen warships. His intention was to pacify the war-torn Western Isles and their clan chiefs. After visiting Duntulm Castle, the fleet sailed around the north of the island and anchored in what was then known as Loch Chaluim Chille, where the clan chiefs had been told to gather to pay respect to their liege lord. It would appear that this wasn't the solemn occasion it was meant to be. Accounts of the time tell of people travelling from all over the island to see the spectacle and enjoy the carnival atmosphere that ensued. Everyone was so impressed that it was decided that the event should be written in the annals of history by changing the name of the town from Kiltaraglen (the cell (cill) of Talorgan) to Port an Righ, the King's Harbour. And so the name of Portree lives on…

The crofting landscape of the Braes

Portree – a row of colourful buildings at the harbour

I guess Portree has a better ring to it, more appropriate for modern tourism – add a royal connection to your town or village and it suddenly finds itself on the tourist map, but long before the great god of tourism waved his magic sceptre over the town Portree became a port for people leaving the island, rather than visiting it. In the eighteenth century it was a common sight to see the bay full of ships bound for North America, carrying highlanders to a new life, the victims of overpopulation and dire poverty. In 1773 James Boswell, the erudite companion of the blusterous Samuel Johnson, wrote: "Last year when the ship sailed from Portree for America the people on shore were almost distracted when they saw their relations go off. This year not a tear is shed. The people on the shore seemed to think they would soon follow." He was right, mass emigration was almost inevitable. The following century, in 1846, the potato blight arrived in Skye, heralding the beginning of another mass evacuation from the island through Portree. The Highland Clearances didn't miss Skye either and during the next 50 years a large percentage of Skye's population emigrated to North America or Australia.

By the end of the century things had improved, thanks to the popularity of coal-fired steamships. Daily steamer services ran between Skye and Strome Ferry, Ullapool, Oban, Lochinver and Stornoway and Tarbert in the Western Isles. The age of Victorian tourism had arrived, and Skye with its scenery, history and folklore was a popular destination for the Victorian romantics.

Modern Portree offers everything a passing-through backpacker could want, other than a proper outdoor shop. I remember there was one, in Wentworth Street, until a number of years ago, but if you're looking for tent pegs, or a new stove, or a new pair of Gore-Tex fabric waterproof trousers to cope with Skye's rainy climate then forget it. Having said that you can buy midge repellent virtually anywhere... We pitched our tent on the very pleasant though midge-infested campsite at Torvaig, then wandered down the road into Portree. Our plan was to treat ourselves to a decent meal, get the car, with our clean clothes and extra food, from the car park, then drive back up the hill to the campsite. Next morning we would travel in comfort into Portree again, leave the car at the free car park and start walking south to The Braes and the rest of our journey.

Sunrise over Portree Bay

Memorial to the Battle of the Braes

I've always been especially fond of Portree, with memories stretching back to the early 1970s when good friends of ours were married in the Free Church there. Rhoda was Portree born and bred and had moved to Glasgow in her late teens to train as a nurse. Her fiancée, Gwyn, was a ship's engineer from Swansea, so the wedding was real mix of Celtic heritage, a blend of Gaelic and Welsh language with the common appreciation of alcohol thrown in for good measure and to help the festivities move along. The high point of the festivities for me came during the church service when the minister, reading from the Scriptures, raised his voice and boomed, "I am the Lord thy God", whereupon a tiny Welsh voice from the somewhere near the back of the kirk answered, "And I am David John Prosser." The young David was only four and had obviously never been subjected to a Free Church sermon before. That wedding went on late into the night, but being a Saturday the festivities reached an untimely end when midnight struck. It was now the Sabbath, and we had to make our way back to our digs for fear of upsetting our Free Presbyterian hosts.

Today Portree is a thriving place, with buses picking up and depositing passengers from all corners of the island in the town's Somerled Square. This central hub is named after a 12th century founder of the Clan MacDonald and it's claimed that it was Sir James MacDonald, a good friend of James Boswell's, who founded the town. Further evidence of Portree's association with the MacDonalds can be found in Wentworth Street (Godfrey Wentworth was the son of the 17th MacDonald chief) and in Bosville Terrace, a family name of the MacDonalds of Sleat.

Fish and chips at the harbour sounded like a good idea and we enjoyed the finest fish supper either of had eaten in a long time. No doubt our appetites had been well and truly whetted by the walking, but the colourful setting of the harbour certainly added extra spice. In a wonderful natural setting, the harbour is cradled by high ground and cliffs with views across the bay to the tiered crags of Ben Tianavaig. We sat, happy and content, with our legs dangling over the edge of the harbour wall, watching the fishing boats, the pleasure craft, the seagulls and the comings and goings of tourists and locals alike. There's a story I once heard about an old Skye man who was being interviewed about the tourism industry and the huge number of people who visit Skye in the summer. "What I don't understand," he said, "is why they don't just stay at home and send their money?" It's a sentiment shared by fewer Skye folk these days, many of whom augment their crofting way of life with a summer job in the tourism industry.

Next morning, having left the car in the car park again, we shouldered our packs and made our way out of Portree. In recent years the town has spread out from its traditional centre, with newer buildings including housing, supermarkets and the island's main secondary school. Also on the southern outskirts of Portree is the Skye Heritage Centre and its associated Aros Experience, designed to bring to life the history and experience of Skye. There has been a longstanding exhibition in the Centre about sea eagles and I was keen to see it. Only the day before, as we tramped along the ridge just below Ben Dearg my attention was taken by something below me. From above it was clear that this was a big bird – an eagle perhaps, and it wasn't long before its white wedge-shaped rump gave it away. It was a sea eagle. Even at a distance of a couple of hundred metres there was no doubting the power of the raptor as it flew out from the corrie, wings held firm, the tips widely fingered.

As it flew away from us I followed it through my binoculars and I soon saw that it wasn't alone. Another sea eagle was spiralling above the outer recesses of the corrie and now the pair of them soared upwards in the thermals before vanishing from sight over the rim of Ben Dearg's dark ridge. Like our experience with the Minke whales we were left exuberant, thrilled to see such magnificent creatures so close at hand.

The Isle of Skye has for long been a stronghold of the sea eagle. A number of years ago I made a radio programme about sea eagles with the naturalist John Love. In the mid 1970s, sea eagle chicks were brought over from Norway and released on the Isle of Rum, at that time owned by the Nature Conservancy Council Scotland (the island is now owned by NCC's successor body, Scottish Natural Heritage). John played a major role in that reintroduction, releasing young birds that soon made their way north to the Isle of Skye where the first pair attempted to breed in 1987. Since then over 20% of the adult population in Scotland are resident on Skye. I guess the indented coastline, lack of human disturbance and the scattered seabird colonies have all attracted this bird, the greatest of all our raptors. The reintroduction story made a great radio programme, part of a series called 'In the Country' that I presented for BBC Scotland. Indeed, the reintroduction of sea eagles, at the time, was second only in terms of success to the reintroduction of ospreys in the Cairngorms in the 1950s. Since then we've seen a successful return of red kites and, on a much more limited scale, attempts at reintroducing beavers.

The sea eagle became extinct in Scotland in the early 20th century, exterminated by Victorian persecution and egg collectors. The exhibition at the Aros Experience suggests the last white-tailed eagle to be seen on Skye was in 1916. Earlier, in 1871, the naturalist R. Gray wrote: "Nearly all the bold headlands of Skye are frequented by at least one pair of sea eagles." Even today, the white-tailed eagle, or sea eagle, is not universally loved and many crofters claim that the birds will take young lambs, although it's difficult to find someone who can give a first-hand witness account of such a killing. There's little doubt that sea eagles will take weak lambs, or carrion, but I was intrigued by a story that John Philips told me about seeing a golden eagle attack sheep on the slopes of Glamaig. He was with a shepherd friend and saw the eagle dive at the sheep, forcing it towards a cliff edge.

Recently in Wester Ross naturalists from Scottish Natural Heritage have been studying the situation by tagging some lambs with tracking devices and monitoring their whereabouts in a bid to gain an insight into lamb predation. When the investigation ended, a report into the study showed that none of the tagged lambs were attacked by eagles. An SNH spokesman said: "The indications on the impact of sea eagles on lambs appear to be low. In fact an analysis of the content of the eagles' nests showed that the most common prey were seabirds." But local crofters weren't convinced, and claimed the five-month project which saw 60 lambs tagged was doomed to failure – because the tags were so big they put the birds of prey off. The crofters had been seeking some kind of compensation for their losses. I'm pretty sure we haven't heard the last of that particular issue. It's well worth a visit to the Aros Experience and the sea eagle exhibition where CCTV cameras give you a first-hand view of eagle chicks in the eyrie. And if you really want to see these marvellous birds, 'flying barn doors' as they were once described, then sail out on one of the viewing boats from Portree harbour where you're likely to see the birds that nest on the cliffs below Ben Tianavaig.

Looking north-east from the lower slopes of Ben Tianavaig

The view south from Ben Tianavaig

Linking the two landscapes of Trotternish and the Cuillin is an area of fertile loveliness known as The Braes, a stretch of coastline that's dominated by the 413m/1355ft Ben Tianavaig. To reach the bridge over the Varragill River and the quiet single-track road that runs south through The Braes we had to either risk life and limb by walking down the edge of the busy A87 road, or nipping over a locked gate to follow the pebbled shores of Loch Portree, an altogether far safer option. If the Skye Trail is ever to receive 'official' status then this is a section where a path would have to made, all the way from Portree south to the bridge that carries the minor road over the river to Peinmore. I must admit that this section of the walk was one that I was dreading. I don't particularly enjoy walking on tarmac roads and from the bridge over the Varragill River to the road end at Peinchorran was a good 10km. I needed a divergence, something to break up the tarmac-bashing.

During numerous sorties to Skye over the years I've gazed longingly at a little hill that dominates this area of The Braes. It rises immediately south of Portree Bay and forms a continuation of the basalt escarpment of Trotternish. Its cliffs are home to a pair of sea eagles and there are wild goats resident on the hill's slopes. It's called Ben Tianavaig, and despite being a mere 413m/1355ft above sea level it's one of the best viewpoints on the Isle of Skye, or so I'm told. Here was a good opportunity to climb the hill, to break up the road walking just a little. The summit of the hill was swathed in cloud so we didn't expect any great views but we were rewarded with a profound feeling of great exposure above the grey-green waters of the Sound of Raasay and a sense that on a good day the ascent of little Ben Tianavaig would be a real classic. Take this hill and transplant it in the Lake District and guidebook writers would be eulogizing about it. Here on Skye it's dwarfed, both physically and aesthetically, by the rugged grandeur of the Cuillin. Nevertheless it's a grand outing for a summer afternoon and there was an otherworldly feel to the tiny crofting hamlet of Camastianavaig as we left the stony beach, with inquisitive seals peering out of the bay at us and an equally inquisitive crofter wondering where we were going. "Take care," he said when I told him where I was heading, "a geologist fell from the cliffs and was killed just last summer."

With his words ringing in our ears we did take care – there are certainly one or two spots where the basalt rock, made treacherously slippery by the rain, could be hazardous and the cliff line that you follow all the way to the summit is, in places, quite exposed. Despite that the route is straightforward, although the mists began to wrap themselves around us like damp, cold tentacles, as we climbed higher. Visibility soon shrunk to a few metres. By the summit trig pillar we were rewarded with a brief opening of the clouds, revealing Portree in its harbour setting away below. Indeed, the hill's name, Tianavaig, means the harbour at the foot of the hill. By the time we returned to Camastianavaig and picked up our route again the day was rolling on and after climbing the hill it was pleasant to stride out along a comparatively flat road, even though it was tarmac.

Marsh orchid

Whether it was an improvement in the weather, or the sense of pastoral softness after the wildness of Trotternish, we both began to enjoy this walk. The road, much of it tree-lined, passed by old croft houses and modern bungalows alike with constant views across the Sound to Raasay and its curious 'volcano' like summit, Dun Caan. The houses make up tiny settlements – Lower Ollach, Upper Ollach, Gedintailor and The Braes itself.

At one point we passed a field where a man in overalls – the classic uniform of the highland crofter – was hard at work. I nodded a greeting to him and he waved back, but as we continued along the road I heard a voice shout "Cammie – is that you?"

Glamaig from Ben Tianavaig

That brought me up short. No-one has called me Cammie since I was a lad. Even Gina was surprised! The man in the overalls was lumbering over the wall from the field, a big man, swarthy and bulky. He towered over me, his face only inches from mine. "Now look at me," he demanded. "Look at me closely, and don't tell me you don't recognize me. And I know you too," he said, pointing his hand at Gina without taking his face an inch away from mine.

I don't know if you've ever been in a position like this but the truth of it is that I'm terrible at remembering faces. I'm even worse at remembering names. Whenever Gina and I go to any kind of gathering I always warn her that if I don't introduce her to someone it's not bad manners, it's just that I can't remember their name. The big man in front of me was smiling, so that was a good sign, and as I gazed at him there was a hint of recognition, but no more than a hint. "I need a clue," I muttered, embarrassed.

"OK, he said, obviously happy to keep the game going. "I knew Gina when she lived in a nurses' flat in Glasgow." That was a good clue. When I first met Gina she was a nurse and I was a young policemen working on the south side of Glasgow. This guy must have been a cop. "Govan Police Office?" I suggested. "Close," he said. "Plantation Police Office – you must remember me, Lorne Nicolson." He put his hand out and it was like shaking hands with a bunch of bananas, except these were bananas with a vice-like grip.

In a flash I remembered. Lorne had joined the City of Glasgow Police force shortly after me and we worked together out of Plantation Police Office in an area of Glasgow's south side that was eventually demolished and replaced with trendy looking flats. In those days tenement life may have been one of deprivation, but there was a community spirit that died when the authorities demolished the old tenements and replaced them with high-rise flats. People were moved out of the city to vast suburban housing schemes – "deserts wi' windaes", as Billy Connolly once famously remarked.

"I've seen you a few times on the telly," said Lorne, "Is this you on another of your big walks?" Briefly I shared our plans with him and as I did so the germ of an idea began to crystallize in my mind. "How long did you stay in the police force?" I asked. "Almost thirty years," he said. "Finished up as a Chief Inspector, and

Ex-policeman Lorne Nicolson

retired a couple of years ago. Decided to come home to Skye and help my old mother run her croft. Her house is just along the road. Why don't I drive along and get her to put the kettle on? It'll be great to catch up." We agreed, and Lorne got into his van and drove on ahead – "You'll see the van in the drive when you get there," he said, leaning out of the window. "Just come in – my mother'll be delighted to meet you both."

As we walked along to the house I shared my idea with Gina. We were very close to the locality where the last battle on British soil took place in 1882. It involved local crofters armed with sticks and stones against 50 policemen who had been sent north from Glasgow to quell a longstanding dispute about grazing rights. The incident caused such strong feeling among the people of Skye that Prime Minister Gladstone eventually set up a Royal Commission to investigate the crofters' grievances. The result of that was a document known as the Napier Report, the blueprint for much of today's crofting legislation. What could be better than to ask an ex-Glasgow police inspector, and a son of The Braes to boot, to tell us the story on our Skye television programme? Would he side with the crofters, or the Glasgow policemen? Over a cup of tea, biscuits and cakes, and after much reminiscing about life as a Glasgow copper, I asked Lorne if he'd be up for it. "Absolutely," he said, "although I might have to do a bit of swotting up." His mother, a delightful grey-haired lady with a kindly twinkle in her eye, whispered slyly to me. "You might not be able to stop him blethering," she said. "That'll be the only problem. When Lorne was born he was inoculated with a gramophone needle!"

Lorne turned out to be the perfect interviewee. I came back to The Braes about a month later and we filmed Lorne sitting by the memorial cairn to the Battle of the Braes with me. This is the gist of what he told me. "The people at the time were in wretched poverty. The herring had gone, there had been a potato blight and there was no money for the sheep. The kelp (seaweed) industry had gone because the Germans had started producing potash so they were reduced from earning £30 a season on the herring fishing to £1."

I asked Lorne to put himself into the position of those policemen of the time. The sergeant says, "I need volunteers to go to Skye and sort out a bit of a crofting argument." Would you have seen it as a bit of a jolly? "Yes, absolutely." Said Lorne. "The mindset of the policemen would have been, great, let's get away from Glasgow for a bit, we'll do our job, we'll march, we'll look good, and we'll do everything right." They marched from Portree, all the way to Braes, arrested the protesters and brought them back to this spot where we're sitting. The Braes folk had prepared for them coming and rolled stones and boulders down the hill on top of the police. It was a real stramash. A few policemen were injured and through time we've come to know it as a battle, but it was really just a skirmish. But the important thing is that the Battle of the Braes was the catalyst that created problems all over the island.

"Do you think the police were surprised at their reception?" I asked. "More than surprised" said Lorne, "I don't think they expected anything like it. I expect they thought they'd come up here, march up the hill and down again, and nothing would happen."

Looking south-east towards the mainland

"As someone who's a crofter, and a retired Glasgow policeman of thirty years standing, where would your sympathies have lain?" I asked. "Basically, my sympathy was with the people, with any people who are downtrodden, but I still have a wee sneaky respect for the cops who came up here. They didn't know what to expect because nobody had told them what could happen. They were simply obeying orders. They came, took a hiding, and went home again."

"What was the outcome of all the unrest that was created by the Battle of the Braes?" I asked Lorne. "The ultimate outcome was the Napier Commission" he explained. "The government brought forward the Crofters Holdings Act of 1886 and crofters got security of tenure – they were able to pass their crofts on to their children. Most of the rents were reduced by 50% and it was probably the best bit of legislation the crofters of Scotland ever had. It was wonderful for the crofters, and I can't help grinning when I think of it, and it's something we have to try and hang on to, and not change the system too much."

Lorne Nicolson is typical of many folk who have left Skye to find work and have returned to their native heath on retirement, some, like Lorne, to work the family croft and others just simply to live out their remaining years on the island of their birth. I suspect many of the smart new bungalows we passed on the road were retirement cottages and certainly the hamlet at the road end, Peinchorran, has that air of retirement about it. Beyond the turning area at the end of the road a signpost points east, to Sligachan, our route for the early evening. We only had 5km or so to walk down the shores of Loch Sligachan to the campsite and the Sligachan Inn, and the midges were already biting. We didn't linger.

Across the sea loch, at Sconser, we watched the ferry leave for Raasay, birthplace of arguably the greatest of Gaeldom's bards. Sorley MacLean (in Gaelic Somhairle MacGill-Eain) was born at Ostaig on the Isle of Raasay in 1911 where his upbringing was rooted in the richness of Gaelic culture. *Hallaig* (named after a place on Raasay) is one of his best-known poems and for years I've been attracted by its underlying themes of nature. Indeed, while much of MacLean's work dwells on the brutality of war and modern exploitation, he often uses landscape as a kind of symbolism. His work doesn't offer much in the way of light reading, and it's been suggested that reading the poetry of Sorley MacLean can feel like a physical work-out.

A lovely footpath parallels the loch shore below the steep, frowning cliffs of the An Leitir ridge of Ben Lee. On the opposite shore the summer evening sun was lighting up the slopes of Glamaig, one of the finest of the Red Cuillin and the scene of the annual Glamaig Hill Race. I've climbed the hill a few times and I know to my cost that the route the fell runners take is notoriously steep. It's incredible that in 1899 a visiting Nepalese soldier by the name of Thapa Ghurka ran to the summit of the 773m/2537ft mountain, and back down again, in 75 minutes. When MacLeod of MacLeod, the landowner, was told about this he refused to believe it so Thapa ran up and down again, this time reducing his time to a phenomenal 55 minutes. That remained the official record right up until the 1980s. The current record, held by Mark Rigby, is 44 minutes and 41 seconds. Astonishing.

"My sympathy was with the people, with any people who are downtrodden, but I still have a wee sneaky respect for the cops who came up here."

Away ahead of us now, forming a jagged silhouette against the sky, was the unmistakable outline of Sgurr nan Gillean and Am Basteir with Sgurr a'Bhasteir hiding the third Munro of that north Cuillin trio, Bruach na Frithe. The ascent of these three Munros makes up one of the finest expeditions in the Cuillin, a mountain range that has no equal in the rest of Britain. We felt tired after a long day but couldn't think of a better finale to what had turned out to be a surprisingly interesting section of the walk, despite the fact that I had initially thought it would have been the low point of the trip. The burn that runs down to the head of Loch Sligachan from Coire Ghaisgeach was thankfully low and we crossed it with dry feet, eager to reach the green sward of the Sligachan campsite where we could put up the tent, and head to the pub for a pint or two and a bar meal.

Sea and distant mountains – archetypal Skye

The camp site was busy when we arrived, and a welcome breeze from the loch kept the midges at bay. As Gina sorted herself out in the tent I went off to take some photographs of the Cuillin from the old Sligachan bridge. I said I'd only be ten minutes but it was to be a good 90 minutes before I returned. As I passed the entrance to the pub who should come out but an old pal of mine, the mountain guide Mick Tighe. He was heading off to Dunvegan to meet a climbing client but suggested we have a quick pint before he left. I should have realized there's no such thing as a quick pint with Mick. He's one of the real characters of Scottish mountaineering and I've known him since the early 1980s. Eventually he said he'd come back to the tent with me and apologize to Gina for holding me up. I told him that wouldn't be necessary but he insisted. He must have seen the look on Gina's face from a distance because he suddenly changed his story and said it was my fault. With a straight face he told Gina it was me who insisted on having a pint or two, despite the fact he was in a hurry to get to Dunvegan. Thanks, pal...

SLIGACHAN TO LOCH CORUISK

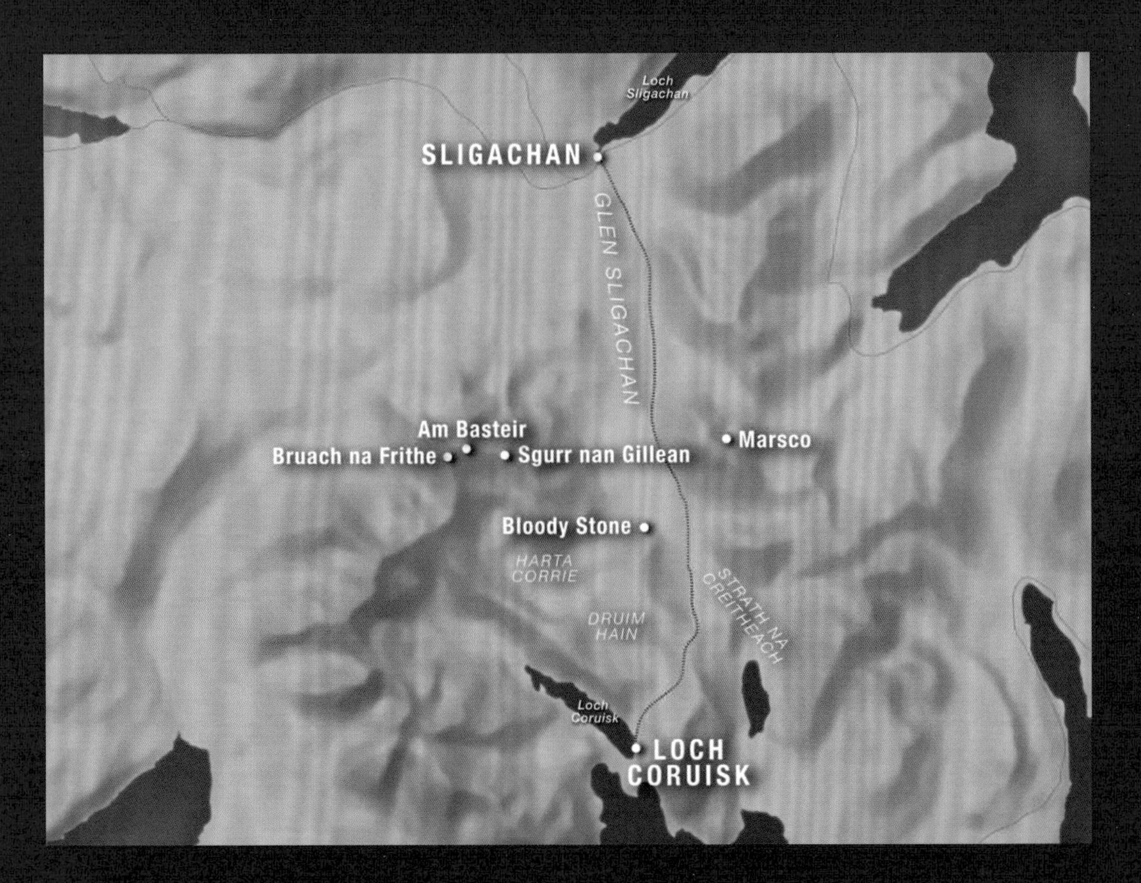

Map
Ordnance Survey 1:50,000 Landranger Sheet 32 (South Skye).

Distance
12 kilometres/7.5 miles.

Approx. time
5-7 hours.

Terrain
Mountain footpaths.

Trail Information

Route

Follow footpath S through Glen Sligachan as far as the path junction just beyond Lochan Dubha. Take the right fork at the junction and follow the path over the shallow bealach between Druim Hain and Sgurr Hain. Descend SW, past Loch a' Choire Riabhaich to the S shores of Loch Coruisk.

Accommodation

Sligachan Hotel: 01478 650204
www.sligachan.co.uk

Excellent and historic hotel. Good food and very interesting museum. Self-catering cottage, bunkhouse and campsite also available.

Sligachan to Loch Coruisk

There are a number of hostelries scattered around the country that could lay claim to being a national cradle of mountaineering. The Pen y Gwryd in North Wales, for example, accommodated the members of John Hunt's team when they trained and planned in 1952 for their successful ascent of Everest the following year, and has a long history of association with climbers. Likewise, Cumbria's Wasdale Head Inn claims to be the birthplace of British rock climbing, where climbers such as Walter Parry Haskett-Smith, the first to ascend Napes Needle in 1886, and Owen Glynne Jones epitomised the era. I suspect the Kingshouse Hotel at the head of Glen Coe, with its associations with early members of the Scottish Mountaineering Club, might want to challenge that assertion.

But for me the cradle of Scottish mountaineering (I wouldn't want to be presumptuous by making claims for England's climbing history) is the Sligachan Inn, here on the Isle of Skye. The present building dates from 1830, when it was moved from its original position near the head of the loch, where it traditionally served cattle drovers and travellers. The first cattle market was held at Sligachan on October 22, 1794 when 1,400 head of cattle and 200 horses and ponies were sold. The tryst was attended by about 400 people – all good business for the Inn. It's said that the tryst was accompanied by a huge tinker encampment at nearby Crossal where song, dance and merriment went on all night long. Sounds a bit like Seumas' Bar today!

Early morning light on the Cuillin

The Sligachan Hotel and campsite

The present hotel has been owned by the Campbell family since the start of the 20th century and I was keen to talk to Mrs Fiona Campbell who runs the hotel today along with her daughter and son-in-law. Unfortunately Mrs Campbell's son Iain had just passed away, so I didn't want to intrude at a sensitive time. Instead I asked her son-in-law Sandy if it would be possible to come back later in the summer and film in the hotel, particularly in the excellent little museum. He didn't think there would be a problem and a few weeks later I did go back with cameraman Dominic and Richard Else who filmed me in the museum talking about one of the most enduring partnerships in Scottish mountaineering, that of Professor Norman Collie and a local crofter, John 'Morton' Mackenzie. Norman Collie achieved a distinction that only one other Englishman, before or since, has achieved. A Scottish mountain, Sgurr Thormaid (Norman's Peak) on the Skye Cuillin, was named after him. Not so far away along the tight contorted ridge another peak, Sgurr Thearlaich (Charles' Peak) is named after a contemporary, Charles Pilkington, later to become President of the London-based Alpine Club.

Although often mistaken as being Scots, J. Norman Collie was born in Manchester in 1859. His father was of Celtic origin – part Scots, part Irish – and his mother Catherine came from a prominent middle class family – her father owned silk manufacturing mills in Manchester. Before the young Norman became a teenager the family business began to flounder and the Collies moved to Bridge of Allan near Stirling, and then to Glassel House on Deeside where Norman's passion for exploration grew into a deep and abiding love of wild places and wild things. A slim lad with aquiline features, he was apparently shy and reserved, happy with his own company although he was particularly close to his elder brother Henry, with whom he was to share many of his future adventures.

Collie enjoyed those youthful years, exploring the woods and fields which surrounded the lowly Hill o' Fare in rural Aberdeenshire. How the memories of those carefree wanderings must have burned in Collie's mind for the next few years of his life, during the events which plunged him deep into despair and depression. His mother hated living in Scotland and missed her literary friends, her artistic soirees and socialising so, as a result, they moved to Clifton near Bristol to be close to the rest of her family. Collie's days of being footloose and fancy-free came to an abrupt end.

He was sent as a boarder to Charterhouse and loathed it – he hated the discipline and the bullying and at one point he even considered drowning himself. But when he was 16, the American Civil War seriously affected the price of cotton, and the family's fortunes crumbled. Norman was taken out of his expensive, fee-paying school and sent to Clifton College as a day student. He didn't particularly shine as a scholar and was eventually asked to leave because he was so bad at classics. It was only later, at University College, Bristol, that he began to blossom as an academic – he studied science under Professor Edmund Letts. In his third year Letts thought so highly of him that he appointed him paid assistant when he took up a new post in Belfast. Collie spent three years in Ireland working closely with Letts and they jointly published two scientific papers. He later became a teacher, a position he didn't particularly enjoy, but it was during this period of his life, in 1886, that he went on an angling holiday with his brother Henry to the Isle of Skye – a vacation that was to radically change his life!

Looking south from Marsco

Uncharacteristically for the Western Isles, the weather was superb, and the long sunny days were too hot for fishing. Instead the Collie brothers climbed some hills, those black gabbro peaks that were to become so familiar in the years to come. It's important to remember that at this time climbing as a sport was very much in its infancy and the whole concept of scrambling your way up a mountain was still a novelty. It was therefore with some surprise that the two brothers were stopped in their tracks by the sight of two climbers high on a crag above them. To Collie, it was a revelation. "I sat with mountaineers hundreds of feet above me, on what appeared to be rocks as steep as the walls of a house. In those days I knew nothing about climbing, and it seemed to me perfectly marvellous that human beings should be able to do such things."

"I sat with mountaineers hundreds of feet above me, on what appeared to be rocks as steep as the walls of a house."

Inspired by what they saw, the Collies got hold of a rope and set off for the Cuillin. To the south-west of the hotel, the bare, rocky walls of Coire a' Bhasteir form an impressive north-facing rampart which is well seen from Sligachan. Bounded on either side by prominent pointed peaks – the magnificent Sgurr nan Gillean on the left and the lower Sgurr a' Bhasteir on the right – it is dominated by its central peak, Am Basteir (the Executioner) and its distinctive 'Tooth'. With the intention of climbing Sgurr nan Gillean (appropriately enough, the Peak of the Young Men), the two brothers set out for the corrie, from where they planned to climb onto the ridge, and then onto the summit. They didn't make it. The narrow ridge and several rocky 'gendarmes' proved too much for them and after several hours of scrambling and scrabbling on the face, they gave up and returned to the inn. They tried again the next day and once more spent many hours trying first to surmount the pinnacles of Sgurr nan Gillean, and finally the peak itself, but for the second time they were defeated. Acting on some local advice, they successfully climbed the mountain on their third attempt – that was their introduction to mountaineering and for Norman, "for the next twenty-five years, mountain climbing became more important to me than fishing..."

A Brocken Spectre on Marsco

A few days later, intoxicated by the heady mixture of mountain ambition, the brothers engaged the help of a local guide, John 'Morton' Mackenzie of Sconser and the three of them climbed Am Basteir, the Executioner. For Norman Collie and John Mackenzie, it was the beginning of a long-standing mountaineering partnership, and for Norman, the genesis of a life-long love affair with the Cuillin. Collie and Mackenzie became firm friends and climbed together every time Collie visited Skye. On each visit he would immediately contact Mackenzie at Sligachan, and the two would formulate their plans for the holiday. The two men, from such different backgrounds and cultures, were bound together by a common love and appreciation of the hills. Even in later years, when Collie was considered to be the accomplished Victorian man, an expert in many fields, wine, food, art, literature, and of course the sciences, his friendship with Mackenzie, if anything, grew stronger. He was aware that in this rough rustic Highlander, there was a great sense of integrity, and an inner strength.

From guiding visitors to local beauty spots, John Mackenzie had very quickly progressed to be a first-rate climber, initially with the Pilkington brothers, who made the first ascent of the Inaccessible Pinnacle of Sgurr Dearg in 1880, with W.W. Naismith, and later with Norman Collie, with whom he climbed for almost half a century. By the time he had given up climbing the hills because of his age, he had shared a rope with many of those who made significant contributions to the development of British climbing. He was held in such esteem that the Alpine Club, in later years, always sent him a complimentary copy of the *Alpine Journal* – a rare privilege indeed, although he was never invited to become a member.

The mountaineer and writer Ben Humble, who lived his later years in Aviemore where he cultivated wild flower gardens at Glenmore Lodge, once described a meeting with Mackenzie in Sconser, just along the road from the inn on the shore of Loch Sligachan, "Later that evening we had the good fortune to fall in with John Mackenzie," he wrote. "We had heard of him, for his name appears in all books on Skye. He is the most famous mountain guide in Britain; a man among men, white-bearded, ruddy complexioned and clear of eye, and though over seventy he was, up till a few years ago, leading the way to the mountain tops. He does not climb now, but is still a mighty fisherman. What a grand life Mackenzie has had!

He has watched the growth of rock climbing in Skye from its infancy, and was with the parties when many of the peaks were first climbed. He was one of the first to climb the Inaccessible Pinnacle of Sgurr Dearg and it is fitting indeed that Sgurr Mhic Coinnich (Mackenzie's Peak) should perpetuate his memory." When they first met Collie was 28 and Mackenzie 31. In later years Collie described him as a lovable, charming and delightful companion. He recognised in the Gael a deep connection with the wild lochs and moors and suggested that as a companion on a long summer day he was perfect. "There was only one John," he wrote, "simple minded, most lovable and without guile."

Bla Bheinn from Garbh Bheinn

Early morning light on Marsco

Norman Collie's love affair with the Cuillin falls into three distinct periods – the early years between 1886 and 1891 during his vacations, between 1891 and 1904 when he visited the island less frequently, but travelled extensively throughout the mountain areas of Britain and abroad, and between 1904 and 1942, during which time he visited the island much more often and eventually went to live there permanently. But it was during this first period that he made his most important climbs and achieved one of the hardest days he had with his new friend John Mackenzie. It's a day that would make all but the strongest modern mountaineers flinch. The pair began at Sligachan and climbed the Bealach na Claic Moire. From the summit of Sgurr a'Mhaidaidh they traversed eight of the major Cuillin peaks, including the Innaccessible Pinnacle by its steep west side. From Sgurr Dearg they traversed around Coire Lagan to Sgurr Alasdair and made a long rough descent of Coir' an Lochain in the dusk to Loch Coruisk.

Now, in complete darkness they ascended the Druim nam Ramh on the north side of Loch Coruisk, descended into Harta Corrie, walked along Glen Sligachan and arrived back at the Inn at midnight. A fair day – and good training for the Himalaya!

By the 1890s, Collie's reputation as a mountaineer and explorer had spread throughout Britain. He climbed with some of the most famous names of the time; Mummery, Slingsby, Hastings and Herman Woolley and his climbing expeditions took him to Norway, the Alps, the Nanga Parbat area of the Himalaya and to every part of highland Scotland. By this time Collie had become a highly successful scientist whose work spanned the latter years of the nineteenth century and continued right up to the 1930s. He was an outstanding chemist; the inaugural Professor of Organic Chemistry at University College, London, the man responsible for constructing the first neon lamp and who, in another first, applied x-ray photographs for surgical purposes. A brilliant scientific brain often merged with his deep love and appreciation of art, an inclination that was well noted by those around him. A colleague, Sir Herbert Jackson, once commented, "Collie, I truly believe that you are far more interested in the colours of the discharges than in the striking phenomena you are recording!"

During Collie's increasingly frequent visits to Skye, he quickly became aware that the Ordnance Survey one-inch to the mile map was wildly inaccurate, despite the fact that it had only been published the year before his first visit. From his earliest climbs Collie began making his own maps and estimating the heights of the summits. When he started to check these heights by means of an aneroid barometer he was astonished by the results. Not only did they differ from the OS readings, as he had expected, they didn't even correspond with his own readings taken a few days earlier. The scientist was challenged! There were two possible sources of error – inaccuracy in the instrument, and rapidly changing atmospheric pressure. To tackle the first, he constructed and designed his own portable mercurial barometer, while for the second he devised a system for using the OS map for a base and keeping to a minimum the time which elapsed between the readings. His survey of the Cuillin established that at least 13 mountains were over 3,000 feet (914m), and more significantly, that the highest point on the Cuillin Ridge was in fact Sgurr Alasdair and not, as had been thought, the Inaccessible Pinnacle of Sgurr Dearg.

The Red Cuillin from Raasay

Collie and Mackenzie climbed Sgurr Dearg and tackled the great basalt prow of the Inaccessible Pinnacle from its short and steep western side. By all accounts they found it hard, and Mackenzie had to take his boots off and climb in his stockinged feet to try and provide better friction on the wet rock. From the narrow confines of the summit perch Collie observed that the summit of Sgurr Alasdair, across Coire Lagan to the south, appeared to be higher, so, on impulse, decided that he had to check it out at once. The resulting traverse, from Sgurr Dearg around the rim of Coire Lagan to Alasdair is a rough day's mountaineering, even by today's standards. Gingerly lowering themselves off the Pinnacle, they had to cross the rocky little peak of An Stac to the neck before the long, narrow and exceedingly steep-sided ridge of Sgurr Mhic Choinnich (subsequently named after Mackenzie, as nearby Sgurr Thormaid – Norman's Peak, was named after Collie) from whose summit a vertical step in the ridge, a prominent feature of the Coire Lagan skyline, was avoided by a series of exposed ledges on the west face.

This route is now recognised and known as Collie's Ledge. A scramble over Sgurr Thearlaich and a short vertical descent landed them in the gap at the head of the Great Stone Shoot, from which the sharp little summit of Alasdair was quickly climbed. Collie's earlier hunch had been correct. Sgurr Alasdair was higher than the Innaccessible Pinnacle by 23 feet!

Later, in the Alpine Club Journal, he described some of the difficulties met on the ridge. "Everything was wrapped in gloom… one seemed cut off entirely from the outer world and the lonely grandeur of the place and the stillness of the night was a thing I have never forgotten. How many mountains we went over and how many feet we climbed it is impossible to say for in many places we traversed backwards and forwards and up and down in our endeavours to overcome the difficulties that we met with on that extraordinary ridge of the Coolin." As he grew older Collie devoted progressively more time to the Isle of Skye and virtually every summer from 1912 he rented a house at Glen Brittle, which he shared with his friend, the artist Colin Philip, under the shadow of the Cuillin's imposing jagged peaks. When John Mackenzie died in 1933 Collie, aged 74 but still active, walked alone to the summit of Am Basteir and declared that this would be his last climb.

At the outbreak of the Second World War Collie was an isolated and taciturn figure haunting the Sligachan Inn; a new order was beginning with climbers seeking out newer and harder routes in the Cuillin and, in doing so, bringing to a close the golden age of exploratory climbing. A young RAF pilot on sick leave, Richard Hillary, was one of the last to see Collie alive. He made this note in his diary: "We were alone in the inn, save for one old man who had returned there to die. His hair was white but his face and bearing were still those of a great mountaineer, though he must have been a great age. He never spoke, but appeared regularly at meals to take his place at a table, tight-pressed against the windows, alone with his wine and memories. We thought him rather fine." Norman Collie died in Skye in 1942 and was buried in the tiny cemetery at Struan alongside his closest friend John Mackenzie of Sconser. The memory of both pioneers lives on in the Cuillin in two peaks, which stand firmly astride the narrow, winding ridge. Sgurr Thormaid and Sgurr Mhic Coinnich, Norman's Peak and Mackenzie's Peak are testimony to two men of different cultures, bound together in their common love of these magnificent mountains of the Isle of Skye.

I don't think there's any finer testimony to the Cuillin than some words that Norman Collie had published in the 1897 edition of the Scottish Mountaineering Club Journal in which he wrote movingly of this affection he had for these wild, western mountains: "…when the wild Atlantic storms sweep across the mountains; when the streams gather in volume, and the bare rock faces are streaked with the foam of a thousand waterfalls; when the wind shrieks amongst the rock pinnacles, and the sky, loch, and hill-side is one dull grey, the Coolin can be savage and dreary indeed; perhaps the clouds towards evening may break, then the torn masses of vapour, tearing in mad hunt along the ridges, will be lit up by the rays of the sun slowly descending into the western sea, 'robing the gloom with a vesture of diverse colours, of which the threads are purple and scarlet, and the embroideries flame'; and as the light flashes from the black rocks, and the shadows deepen in the corries the superb beauty, the melancholy, the mystery of these mountains of the Isle of Mist will be revealed."

There's an Ossianic feel to that quote, a Celtic sense of mystery that, for me, sums up the essence of the Cuillin. Indeed, it's here, on these steep-sided mountains closest to Sligachan that, like Norman Collie, I've experienced some of the finest and most memorable hill days of my life. One particular occasion stands out, partly because it wasn't planned in any great detail. It was a day snatched from between two bouts of filming when we were making our Wilderness Walks BBC series on Skye. On one of our 'rest days' I climbed the Sligachan Munro trio with a friend from Cumbria, David Powell-Thomson, a strong fell runner and experienced climber. David had never been to Skye before and I think this was the key – I suspect I caught something of his excitement as we scampered up the length of the Fionn Coire between Sgurr a' Bhasteir and Bruach na Frithe. The dark walls of the mountains on either side of us pressed in as we climbed higher over seas of rock and boulder scree. It didn't take us long to reach the crest of the ridge, and we wandered up towards the summit of Bruach na Frithe rejoicing in the Alpine-like surroundings. David had never, in his own words, seen anything to compare with this view of the Cuillin ridge.

"…a vesture of diverse colours, of which the threads are purple and scarlet, and the embroideries flame; and as the light flashes from the black rocks, and the shadows deepen in the corries the superb beauty, the melancholy, the mystery of these mountains of the Isle of Mist will be revealed."

Am Basteir was next so we retraced our steps to the Bealach nan Lice and followed the rough path round the foot of Am Basteir to the Bealach am Basteir where the normal route climbs up the rocky ridge to the summit, dropping at one point into a narrow recess which calls for a fairly agile bit of scrambling, or an abseil if you have a rope. This gap in the ridge has been made worse by a rockfall and many Munro-baggers now avoid it by following a series of ledges on the south side of the ridge.

Nicholson's Chimney, a steep 25-metre gully, offers access to Sgurr nan Gillean's west ridge which would lead to our third summit. The ascent is probably more of a rock climb than a scramble but we went for it anyway, even though we weren't carrying a rope or any of the accoutrements of the rock climber. Instead we relished the big solid holds in the steep chimney and delighted in the narrow, steep and sinuous ridge crest that took us to the summit of the mountain. This has to be the finest mountain summit in the country, an airy crest thrown up by steep rocky slopes on all sides. It was no wonder that notable Skye-based scribe, Sheriff Alexander Nicolson, once described it as "the great upheaval of Sgurr nan Gillean." It was David's 50th birthday, and he reckoned it was the best birthday of his life.

That's the effect the Skye Cuillin can have on you and of course the great challenge for hillwalkers, and nowadays fell-runners, is to complete the whole ridge, including its eleven Munros, inside 24 hours. While most hillwalkers will take much of those 24 hours to tackle the sinuous ridges, scrambles and climbs between Sgurr nan Eag and Sgurr nan Gillean, super-fit fellrunners complete it in much faster times. Indeed, the current 'record' is held by runner Es Tressider, who is also, not surprisingly, an accomplished mountaineer, in an astonishing 3 hours, 17 minutes and 28 seconds. Es has described the day of his record-breaking run as "one of the most spectacular I've ever seen. The valley was slowly enveloped in a sea of mist, leaving the ridge the only thing floating above in the sunshine. It was like running in heaven."

Gina and I set off from Sligachan on a morning of dazzling beauty. A glorious sunset the evening before heralded good things for the day and we weren't disappointed. Our route lay to the south, down the long miles of the Sligachan Glen with the Black Cuillin rearing up on our right. On the opposite side of the glen the view was dominated by a much smaller and less celebrated hill.

Beyond the Druim Ruaige face of Beinn Dearg Mhor, Marsco rises as a rough pyramid, its western ridge bulging out into a curious protuberance called Fiaclan Dearg, the red tooth. It's a bold mountain, a distinctive shape that dominates what is one of the finest views in Scotland. Marsco – the name comes from the Norse, not unusual in the Skye of the Viking raiders and settlers, and means 'seagull mountain' – is neither a Munro nor a Corbett, but you have to climb its full 736m/2414ft from sea level. It is, however, in elevated company. Just south lies the brooding notched ridge of Clach Glas and Bla Bheinn, a great wall of spires, gullies and buttresses. On a day of storm cloud the rock architecture looks dark and forbidding, like the pass that separates it from its neighbouring Cuillin. This Bealach na Beiste, the Pass of the Monster, was where MacKinnon of Strath long ago grappled with and slew a fearful beast.

The Sligachan River in winter

Time for a break in Glen Sligachan

I first climbed Marsco with Donnie Munro, not long retired from the folk-rock band Runrig and contemplating a political career. Donnie was guesting in one of my Wilderness Walks television programmes and despite the fact he had performed a song called *Nightfall on Marsco* he had never actually climbed the hill and was keen to do so. While Marsco can be climbed more easily from the head of Loch Ainort in the east, this longer approach down Glen Sligachan gave us the opportunity to actually climb the peak by one route, and descend by another. This way you are more aware of the hill's commanding position, and its individuality, rather than experiencing it as part of the long Red Cuillin ridge that runs from Bla Bheinn in the south to Glamaig in the north.

A well-used path runs down Glen Sligachan for about 3km to reach the Allt na Measarroch. A narrower path then follows the north bank of the burn and climbs steadily up to the grassy slopes of the Mam a'Phobuill, the pass of the people, which is the high point in an old trade route between the head of Loch Ainort and Glen Sligachan. From the top of this pass grassy slopes climb south into Coire nan Laogh and then up the corrie's north-east ridge to a high col between the summit ridge and the hill's south-east top. From this high bealach the summit ridge tapers off to the north-west, gradually narrowing over half a kilometre to a superbly narrow roof-top ridge that leads to the summit cairn and one of the finest views on Skye. Across the gulf of Glen Sligachan the sight of the Black Cuillin simply took our breath away, and to the south Bla Bheinn and Clach Glas left us with little chance of catching it again!

Gina and I were taking a simpler route this morning, and we were in for an easy stroll after our exertions of the day before. The plan was to wander down the length of Glen Sligachan and then, beyond Lochan Dubha, cut over the bealach between Druim Hain and Sgurr Hain before dropping down past Loch a'Choire Riabhaich to the great rocky cauldron that holds the atmospheric Loch Coruisk, one of the wildest, roughest, most awe-inspiring places you could hope to see. We wandered down the glen in no great hurry – we hadn't planned a long day and we were keen to spend some time by Loch Coruisk but we were equally keen to soak in the atmosphere of this superb glen, dominated by not just one great mountain range but two. To the right is the Black Cuillin, with the great rock buttresses of Sgurr nan Gillean, and its pointed peak standing sentinel above the path.

Sunrise over the mainland

On the opposite side lies the Red Cuillin, with the ruddy slopes of Glamaig and Marsco contrasting strongly with the streaky darkness of Sgurr nan Gillean, a testament perhaps to their different origins. Away at the head of the glen, like outliers from the main Black Cuillin ridge, lay the castellated form of Clach Glas and Bla Bheinn, two magnificent mountains that share the qualities of their western neighbours, but appear to have been abandoned by them, two mountains whose loss is our gain, for the view from Bla Bheinn towards the Black Cuillin is one of the most awe-inspiring in Scotland.

Soon the curved recess of the Harta Corrie opened up on our right, the rocks reflected in the waters of Lochan Dubha. The call of a black-throated diver rose to meet us, a mournful wail that could have been the embodiment of events that occurred here in the past. Not far from us, below the flanks of Meall Dearg, lay the site of a fierce encounter that took place between the Macdonalds and the Macleods in 1601.The clansmen apparently fought the entire day and the legends claim that only one person, a Macleod, was left standing as afternoon turned to night. The bodies of the slain were all piled up around a 10-metre high boulder that became known as the Bloody Stone, or the Rock of the Flaying. It was the last battle between these two great clans.

Close by Lochan Dubha the footpath splits – one path continues through Strath na Creitheach, passes along the shores of Loch na Creitheach and eventually reaches Camasunary while the other climbs over the Druim Hain ridges and drops into Coruisk. We took the latter. A fairly stiff climb up the badly eroded path brings you to the high point of the pass and at this point the views have you reaching for the camera. Bla Bheinn appears as a long and gentle ridge rising to a rounded summit, its darkness contrasting with the pink slopes of its close neighbour Garbh-bheinn. To the north Sgurr nan Gillean looks more pointed and pinnacled than ever and for the first time I could begin to discern some meaning behind Sorley MacLean's long poem, *An Cuillin*. I think it's fair to say that a lot of Sorley MacLean's work is pretty abstract, painfully so sometimes, but a sense of meaning can be glimpsed when you realize how often he uses landscape as a kind of symbolism.

According to Meg Bateman, a MacLean scholar and a lecturer at Sabhal Mor Ostaig, Skye's Gaelic medium college, it's the landscape that gives form and sensuousness to MacLean's ideas and lets him communicate them as emotion. In *An Cuillin*, for example, the mountains appear as many different things but essentially the poem traces man's oppression of man, particularly in the context of the Highland Clearances. The ghosts of the perpetrators of the Clearances appear in a demonic dance, perched on the pinnacles. The cries of the people leaving the land are heard. The Cuillin responds, rocking and shrieking. Later, the Cuillin takes on the embodiment of a castrated stallion and the bogs in the glens below represent the spreading of corruption throughout the world. It's heavy stuff, but eventually the human spirit prevails and men gather on the hill to witness the Cuillin taking on the form of a stag, a lion, a dragon and finally an eagle. A triumphant finale. Human dignity rises over adversity, part of the socialist dream that MacLean believed in so fervently. The Cuillin rises, as MacLean writes, on the other side of sorrow.

"Who is this, who is this in the night of the heart?

It is the thing that is not reached

The ghost seen by the soul

An Cuillin rising over the sea"

The classic view of the Cuillin from Elgol

It's hard to deny the permanence of the mountains, their steadfastness, their constant presence, looming over the conceits of man whether in the bloody clan battles or the intolerance and viciousness of the Clearances. MacLean taps into that awareness of longevity and portrays the mountains as a symbol of triumph. In another poem he refers to the Cuillin as "the mother-breasts of the world, erect with the universe's concupiscence." These, are, above all others, the mountains of the Gael.

We stopped at the summit of the pass and sat by some rocks that had been smoothed and polished by the glacier which once eased its grindingly slow way down from here into the loch. Around us the mystery of wildness lay inscrutable and implacable, mountains gaunt and black and slightly sinister in their own strength and anonymity.

We give them names – we even name them after pioneer mountaineers – but in truth they are nameless, as old as time itself, enduring and undefiled. I smiled at the thought. What did Cuchullin or Fionn MacCumhail or Ossian or any of those other ancient warriors think of these mountains. Did they give them names? Did the ancient heroes climb to the sharp summits, did they scramble along the knife-sharp ridges; did they clamber up the shifting screes as we do today? Did these ancient warriors see the mountains as things of beauty, the domain of a natural world from which so many of us are nowadays divorced?

As we made our way down the rough track that drops into the Coruisk basin something curious happened. It was as though the scenery and the peace and the lasting beauty had allowed my mind to open up and in astonishing clarity I recalled some of the old tales of our Celtic heritage. By the time I reached the shore of the loch, the waters calm and black, it was as though I had come into the stronghold of Cuchullin himself. And when you think of the peaks that virtually surround this loch, you think of hillwalking and first ascents and record-breaking runs across the ridge and it all seems so unimportant, and it's good just to sit at the water's edge and soak in the atmosphere of the place, probably the grandest and most inspiring place in the whole of Eilean a'Cheo. The ancient Celts believed water had a special magic as a symbol of vitality and inspiration. A pool of water, or a lochan, could capture the light, as in the reflection of the setting sun for example, and since this couldn't be rationally explained it was believed water had supernatural properties. Wells and springs were charged with magic powers and lakes and rivers were the home of water-horses or sprites or ghosts, as in the *Lady of the Lake*. Could this be the secret of Coruisk? What magic drifts across the evening calm, what creatures dwell in the black waters? Beyond the rocky barriers the choppy waves of Loch Scavaig were flashing emerald green near the shore, the waves capped with tiny white horses. It was going to be a windy night, but that could have been the outcome of a wish I made as I sat beside the rocky pool. A wind to keep the notorious Skye midges at bay. The Coruisk magic was working!

"The ancient Celts believed water had a special magic as a symbol of vitality and inspiration."

Loch Coruisk from Sgurr na Stri

Someone once described Loch Coruisk as "a waste, wild world, not yet out of chaos, nor yet approven of God." There is certainly something otherworldly about it. Sir Walter Scott described it in grandiose terms: "...we found ourselves in a most extraordinary scene; we lost sight of the sea almost immediately after we had climbed over a low ridge of crags, and were surrounded by mountains of naked rock, of the boldest and most precipitous character. The ground on which we walked was the margin of a lake, which seemed to have sustained the constant ravage of torrents from these rude mountains... The proper name is Loch Corrisken, from the deep corrie or hollow, in the mountains of the Coulin, which affords the basin for this wonderful sheet of water."

We camped close to that wonderful sheet of water, by the cascading Scavaig River that connects Loch Coruisk with the sea, and spent the evening walking round this most remarkable loch. Before we did though, I wanted to take a look at three yachts that were moored in Loch na Cuilce, at the head of Loch Scavaig. As we sat on the shore and admired the slim lines of the craft there was some turmoil in the water. To our surprise, and to the surprise of the people on the yachts, three bottle-nosed dolphins broke the surface and spent a good five minutes gamboling and cavorting around the boats. Another little bit of Skye magic…

Friends often wonder at our sanity when we tell them about our backpacking trips. "But what do you do when you camp in the evenings after walking all day?" they ask," How do you spend your time?" We look at each other with a smile before answering. "We usually go for a walk." It's one of the peculiarities of backpacking. While some backpackers, like my good friend Chris Townsend, one of the most prolific long distance backpackers in the world, relish the camping aspect of the activity, Gina and I tend to enjoy the walking, provided the weather is reasonably good. We'd had a fairly easy day so far and since we were in one of the most remarkable places in these islands we were going to make the most of it. Gina hadn't been to Coruisk before, and I suspect by her silence she was pretty stunned. But that silence might have been down to something else.

As we had earlier descended the path to Coruisk, Gina was lagging behind me by about 50 metres or so when I noticed another walker had caught up with her and they appeared to be deep in conversation. The other walker, a young man, eventually passed me with a cheery nod and it wasn't until Gina caught up with me that I realized something was on her mind. The young man apparently worked on the tourist ferry that plies its trade between Elgol and Coruisk and this was his day off. The ferry had dropped him off at Camasunary and he had walked over Sgurr na Stri en route to the pier at the head of Loch Scavaig. He had asked Gina where we were heading and she had told him we'd be camping overnight before heading for Camasunary and Elgol tomorrow. "Over the Bad Step?" he asked. "Yes," said Gina, "what's it like?"

"Mmm," said the lad, "Put it this way, my partner is an extreme rock climber and there's no way she would cross it. In fact our ferry is normally full of hill-walkers who have retreated from it. It's really scary."

Loch Coruisk, the heart of the Cuillin

With that he proceeded to tell her the times the ferry would be running in the morning then took off down the hill, leaving poor Gina more than a little perplexed. I could understand her state of mind. I'd told her earlier she'd have no difficulty crossing the Bad Step, a notorious rock slab that can only be crossed by scrambling along a narrow crack high above the waters of Loch Scavaig, but experience has taught Gina to be a tad circumspect of my advice. In my own defence I sincerely believe she has more ability than she thinks she has, and I try to encourage her by telling her she's more than capable of crossing the likes of the Bad Step, but having said that, a couple of broken ankles in recent years, including one caused by a slip on ice at 17,000 feet on a high pass in the Annapurna Himalaya, has dented her confidence a little.

The Bad Step lies just over 400m south of Loch Coruisk, so I comforted Gina a little by telling her that we would have a look at it in the morning and if she didn't fancy it we could return to the pier and take the ferry to Elgol. It was obvious to me the young man she had met on the trail was simply trying to get a couple of extra fares for his ferry. Damn him! The Bad Step wasn't that bad – or was it?

Bla Bheinn

Map
Ordnance Survey 1:50,000 Landranger Sheet 32 (South Skye).

Distance
12 kilometres/7.5 miles.

Approx. time
6-8 hours.

Terrain
Rough mountain footpaths, some scrambling.

Trail Information

Route

Stay E of the river and go through a narrow defile on a path that follows the shores of Loch nan Leachd. Cross the Bad Step and continue S and SE to Rubha Ban. Follow the shore until you can safely cross the Abhainn Camas Fhionnairigh. Pass the bothy and head E to the buildings at Camasunary. Follow the Abhainn nan Leac NE then climb the SSW ridge of Bla Bheinn to the S summit. Descend by a steep path into a narrow defile then climb to the trig point and summit of Bla Bheinn. Return to S summit and descend steep slopes to the head of Coire Uaigneich. Follow badly eroded footpath NE then E to descend beside the Allt na Dunaiche to the B8083.

BLA BHEINN

Backpacking – putting camping gear into a pack, hoisting it on your back and heading off to some wild land, or a long distance trail for a few days or a few weeks. It's an activity that embraces simplicity – what could be simpler than walking all day, then sleeping all night to get up in the morning and walking all day again? And what could be finer than waking in the morning and seeing the waters of Loch Coruisk through the door of a tent?

While there's an attraction in such simplicity, I would argue that backpacking is considerably more complex than that. The American existentialist Henry David Thoreau once wrote: "I went to the woods because I wished to live deliberately, to front only the essential facts of life, and see if I could not learn what it had to teach, and not, when I came to die, that I had not lived." For most folk, Thoreau's 'woods' suggest a place in which to experience the natural world, a world of mountains, rivers, forests and flowers. Woods or wilderness, wild land or green world, the nomenclature is unimportant; the vital issue is that within that world we can enjoy peace and beauty, space and silence, far away from the stresses and strains of everyday life. Such places have a deep significance not only for those who seek recreation but for mankind itself. Ever since I was a teenager I've rock climbed, climbed mountains, rode a bike and canoed, but predominantly I walk, with passion and relish, as often as I possibly can. And much of that walking has been done with a pack, containing all my needs for several days, on my back.

Bla Bheinn across Loch Slapin

Western seas from Bla Bheinn

Backpacking is all about exposing yourself to the 'natural world', entering it with respect, minimizing your impact on it, treating it on its own terms and not trying to urbanize it, walking for several days, or weeks, carrying in a pack on your back everything you need for survival. It does not rely on porters or pack animals, nor does it rely on wheels or engines. Having said that, backpacking involves, a tad hypocritically but to a degree that the individual backpacker can choose, a dependence on technology. Our lightweight camping stoves are infinitely more efficient and less environmentally damaging than a campfire. Our packs and tents and clothing are a triumph of technology and we salve our green conscience by wearing base layers and fleece jackets recycled from plastic bottles, or more recently, from bamboo, but I'm happy to let others describe the gear. For the moment I want to discuss something more essential than the equipment we carry with us.

As a species, modern mankind is far removed from the outdoor-dwelling abilities of our forefathers. A couple of hundred years of urban living have denied us an inheritance that should naturally have been ours – the ability, to use a rather over-exploited phrase, to commune with nature. Walking and camping and living in high places, or in deserts, or along remote shorelines, or deep in a forest, no longer come naturally to us, and the skills to allow us to do so must be re-learned. We have to re-learn to use our legs, our lungs and our hearts again. We must learn, with the aid of modern contrivances, to navigate, to forecast weather, to find the best places to sleep at night. We must learn, almost conversely, to rid ourselves of the mental and physical shackles that luxurious living has lumbered us with. The essence of a successful backpacking trip is not in what we carry on our backs but in the things we see, the feelings we experience, and in the sounds we hear. The miracle gear we carry allows us to enjoy those things without any degree of masochism but therein lies a trap – the dividing line between a high level of comfort at night in the tent and a high comfort level during the day when you have to carry all the gear. That line is extremely tenuous. Practice and experience allow us to navigate it with a degree of success.

Many of us are aware that wild country has an almost mystical ability to inspire and refresh us. "Climb the mountains and get their good tidings," said John Muir. For all those "bound by clocks, almanacs… and dust and din" and limited to places where "Nature is covered and her voice smothered", Muir claimed wilderness was essential, so much so that, in an obvious plagiarism of the words of Thoreau (*In wildness is the preservation of the world*) he claimed; "In God's wildness lies the hope of the world – the great, fresh, unblighted, unredeemed wilderness". And although we lack that kind of wilderness that Thoreau and Muir might have referred to, we do have a fair amount of wild land in the UK, land that is relatively pristine and unspoiled. We can still find renewal in the stillness of a forest, or on a wind-scoured mountain top – the drift of cloud against the sky, the movement of sun and shadow, the warbling liquid call of a curlew, the flight of an eagle – all these things exist and we can benefit from them, enjoy them, appreciate them, and all because they speak to us of eternal values, things that have always been, as ancient as the duration of days. And all of them; the flight of a bird, the sound of wind surf in the trees, the beauty of a sunset, are completely and utterly unplanned – none of these things have been previously rehearsed, or arranged or planned by man. And that, I believe, is the important issue.

Over the past century our steady urbanisation has also ensured a steady divorce of our physical lives from the natural world so that we no longer consider ourselves a part of it. We climb hills and mountains as though we were strangers, 'conquering' nature to achieve our aims and purposes. It was Carl Gustav Jung's belief that the crisis of our modern world has two root causes; one is this divorce of our physical lives from the natural world, so that we no longer feel part of it; the other is the over-development of our rational, analytical consciousness at the expense of the instinctive, intuitive side of ourselves that is expressed in dreams, myth, fantasy and art. According to Jung we have become cut off from both inner and outer nature. We've lost trust in our traditional faiths and in doing so the spiritual side of our nature has been subdued. The resultant loss of meaning in the lives of many people is reflected in statistics for depression, suicide and mental illness.

Backpacking offers us a route back into both inner and outer nature by allowing us to 're-connect' with the land, to re-learn something of its ways, to reflect on the patterns of life around us, and how we interact with them. Wild land 'connection' is about casting aside the traditional notion that man is dominant and that everything in nature has been designed for man's welfare or pleasure. Paradoxically, this connection often comes in a sudden revelation of our own insignificance when compared with the more lasting reality of mountains, forests and star-studded skies. A bear encounter can have a curiously humbling effect on us and an Alpine electric storm can portray a force and a power that is way beyond humankind's ability to reproduce. Even the sense of savage grandeur in a place like the Loch Coruisk basin can leave us awestruck and inspired.

Indeed, it was here on the Isle of Skye that I first experienced this sense of wild land connection. Having negotiated the moving screes of the Great Stone Shoot above Coire Lagan I reached the jagged crest of the Cuillin on Sgurr Alasdair, where I experienced such a combination of ecstasy and relief that I could exalt in the wild surroundings in a way that could only be described as euphoric. In that heightened state brought on by a combination of emotion, endorphin flow and adrenaline, for the first time in my life I felt at one with the mountain. In a very profound way I had become aware that I wasn't simply a visitor casually climbing some scree and rock – I was part and parcel of the *fabric* of the mountain, the rock, air, water and light. For the first time I experienced a sense of *kinship* with that wild and inhospitable landscape. I had connected with the mountain and, in a sense, transcended my own being.

Descending from Bla Bheinn

Is it possible to 'connect' with the landscape on a day walk? Do you need two or three days or more to achieve this state of mind? I guess I can only comment on a personal level but I certainly need the time and space of two or three days at least to break free of those avalanches of thoughts and worries and concerns that tumble around in my mind when I walk. A one-night sortie at the weekend can often refresh me and purge away a clutter of problems that I had thought might be insurmountable, but I need more time before my mind, loosened by space and solitude, swings open fully and allows that connection to take place. It's at this point we can be led into thinking that backpacking is the panacea for all the various problems that surround everyday living. It's not; it's only a short-term release from those problems, but it does teach us how to cope with them better. It's also worth remembering that the wilderness, or wild land environment, is rarely problem-free in itself. Even amid the freedom and fresh air some of those concerns can take on leviathan proportions and appear almost insurmountable. It's as though we trade one set of concerns and worries – the usual conflicts about work and domestic matters - for another set of problems, albeit concerns of a simpler and less complex nature, problems that are usually conquerable. And that, of course, is the critical factor.

Backcountry problems don't usually require a time-consuming consultation process to work them out. They don't need timetables, schedules or almanacs. You don't have to make appointments with lawyers, advisers or doctors to solve these particular problems. They are usually the simple day-to-day domestic concerns that man has faced since time immemorial – finding a flattish piece of ground to camp on, finding water to drink and avoiding danger – what the writer Colin Fletcher once referred to as grappling with the tangible instead of wrestling with the abstract! But such simple concerns are made no less serious by the knowledge that you can deal with them. They still exist, they still niggle away in the dark recesses of your mind, but experience helps enormously. It teaches you how to fix the problems, and the more trips you undertake the more you realize how easily the little fears and uncertainties can grow out of proportion. Your fretting becomes less overwhelming with the years but the syndrome is still there. We just learn to control it. I'm always amazed that my memories of particular trips are diametrically opposite to some of the fears and concerns I had noted at the time. It seems that in retrospect, even the bad times were good.

An earlier crossing of the Bad Step with former lead singer of Runrig, Donnie Munro

Here, in the wonderful setting of the Cuillin of Skye, Gina and I had allowed the potential problem of the Bad Step to grow in our minds into some kind of monster.

I knew the Bad Step wasn't difficult, a mild scramble, but could Gina cope with it? I had wakened in the wee small hours in the darkness of the tent, turning the thought over in my mind, making myself restless with the fear of a problem that really wasn't there. Eventually, as daylight replaced the gloom of night, I slipped out of my sleeping bag, dressed and headed out along the Camasunary track. The Bad Step was only about 15 minutes walk away. I'd check it out and if I thought Gina couldn't cope with it we'd make alternative arrangements, like catching the ferry to Elgol or crossing Sgurr na Stri to Camasunary.

It was very much as I remembered it. An enormous convex slab of rock with a little ramp leading to a narrow crackline. Once across the crack you have to step down into a groove with a thin crack at head height that's just wide enough to get your fingers into. A shuffling movement gets you along the groove before another step down onto a rocky platform and safety. It all sounds reasonable but the problem is the exposure. All this takes place about 8-10 metres above the rising swell of the sea loch, and if you don't have a head for heights then it could easily faze you. I had seen enough and I was sure Gina wouldn't have any difficulty, but I was mildly angry; annoyed that I had allowed a minor problem to grow legs and become a monster; annoyed that the young man from the ferry should scare Gina in this way for the sake of a couple of extra fares on his bloody boat; and annoyed with myself that I hadn't been more confident, more assured in my own memories of the Bad Step.

To be fair, the Scottish Mountaineering Club's *Skye Scrambles* guide describes the *mauvais pas* as a Grade 1/2 scramble, and some notes on various websites and blogs certainly don't suggest it's an easy crossing. "It is a hard trail (Camasunary to Coruisk) requiring good boots, energy and general mountain skills. En route there are a number of bad steps of which the Bad Step itself is probably impassable without some basic climbing skills. Some undoubtedly would prefer to be led up by a rope," says one. Another claims, "The exposure is significant – 40 to 60 feet down to deep and cold water and there is no alternative route. Falling creates further problems as it is a lonely place." Yet another scaremonger describes the route as follows: "I climbed onto the ledge, and traversed easily up a slope and over one exposed step. At the top of the slope the ledge narrowed and was replaced by a fault line descending from the left.

For four feet or so the footholds were only a couple of inches wide and the hand holds non-existent, with a 15 foot drop into the sea and the fault line sloping downwards at 30 degrees. I did this section bumwise, grateful not to be carrying a large pack, then stood up as the fault widened and my feet found purchase on the top of a flake, with good handholds. The flake ended in a steep step down to a narrow platform and safety." To make matters worse, this report goes on to describe how a companion took a higher line across the slab and got into real difficulties. He slipped, tumbled down the slab and only just managed to stop himself from going over the edge into the sea. Perhaps, just perhaps, my worries had been justified.

By the time I returned to the tent Gina was up and about, busying herself with packing away her sleeping bag and insulated mat and collecting her various bits and pieces into small stuff sacks. We cooked and ate breakfast outside, putting off the moment when we'd leave what was for us, the final camp of our trip. The plan was to cross the Bad Step, make our way round to Camasunary, then follow the coastal path to Elgol from where we'd catch a bus to Broadford. From there a connecting bus would take us north again to Portree where we'd collect our car. That night, we'd be back in our own home in Badenoch, the Skye Trail nothing but a memory. I'd be back though, sooner rather than later, with television producer and photographer Richard Else, cameraman Dominic Scott and our safety officer, Paul Tattersall and even at this stage I knew that our eventual Skye Trail wouldn't finish at Elgol but would probably take us over Bla Bheinn to Torrin, then via the lost villages of Skye, Suisnish and Boreraig, then along the Marble Track to Broadford. But that was in the future. For the moment, the Bad Step still loomed ominously.

As we left Coruisk behind and passed through the narrow channel that leads to the head of Loch nan Leachd, a northern bay of Loch Scavaig, I reflected on an old proposal that might have solved Gina's immediate problem, but which surely would have destroyed the remote and inviolate nature of Loch Coruisk. In 1968 the Army had been requested to build a 3km track over the Am Mam from Strathaird to serve the fishing and shooting lodge at Camasunary. This had caused some concern amongst the hillgoing fraternity at the time but what really created an almighty conservation furore was a plan to build a bridge over the Camasunary river, the Abhainn Camas Fhionnairigh, and continue the bulldozed track to Coruisk, blowing up the Bad Step with dynamite in the process!

On the walk-in to Camasunary from the east

The aggrieved mountaineers, who saw the Bad Step as a natural guardian of Coruisk and all its natural wonder, took their case to the Government and eventually won the argument that such a track could encourage inexperienced people into an area where they could get into serious difficulties. Compromise, as usual, won the day. The track from Strathaird to Camasunary was built but the Bad Step was saved for generations of walkers to fret over.

Elgol in autumn colours with Bla Bheinn in the background

The old argument about inexperienced folk going to the hills was voiced quite vociferously in the early twentieth century by a writer called Otta Swire. Ms Swire lived on Skye for some time and eventually died on the island and her book, *Skye – The Island and its Legends* has become a classic. However, after some paragraphs describing the Cuillin she goes into a discourse about the economic difficulties of the crofting life. The reader wonders where she is going with this theme before she drops her customary tolerant and charitable style and blasts into a real rant:

"Into this carefully planned economy comes, every summer, one (and often more) selfish, conceited, and ignorant tourist, who thinks he knows all about climbing but doesn't. (The real climbers and honest learners are a very different kettle of fish.) But the Ignorant One thinks it clever to go off into the Cuchullins without advice or guide. Then comes the mist or he gets lost or sprains an ankle; next comes the appeal, first to those whose livelihood is guiding; will they give up a day (or several) to search for one who would neither employ or consult them? And then, if the foolhardy cannot be found, there comes the appeal to the whole island. Buses run from Portree, Dunvegan, Armadale, bringing searchers from them all; bringing men who must decide either to ignore the needs of their own families (and I mean *needs,* not wishes) or else to leave a fellow man to die slowly and horribly in the hills, if he has met with an accident not already fatal.

"Is it too much to ask those who do not know the Cuchullin to consult some responsible person before they start? To ask: "Is the route they propose a good one? Are there any known difficulties to watch for? Is the weather suitable?" And above all to tell their chosen route to someone and stick to what they have arranged. Then, in mist or in case of accident, they can be easily and quickly found without upsetting the harvesting of many townships."

Some things never change!

Gina danced over the Bad Step as though it wasn't there. I crossed first, then went back to relieve her of her pack. She then followed me across with a look that said "all this fuss about nothing." For the next few kilometres we followed the faint path round the headland of Rubha Ban, crossing some broad slabs of rock and scrambling down a couple of tricky little craggy sections. Away in the distance, past the tawny slopes that fall steeply from Beinn Leacach and Ben Cleat to the sea, we could just make out the white cottages of Elgol. Soon the whitewashed bothy below the south ridge of Bla Bheinn came into view, a popular shelter amongst hillwalkers who come to enjoy the splendid situation of Camasunary, or Camas Fhionnairigh, the bay of the beautiful shieling. It's a quiet, peaceful and tranquil place, but it might not have been that way if Sheriff Alexander Nicolson's great dream had become a reality.

Writing in the nineteenth century, he declared: "Here undoubtedly is the place where, were it Switzerland, would be a Grand Hotel de Blaveinn, a Grand Hotel des Cuchullins and probably also a Grand Hotel et Pension de Camasunary. Why should there not be one there, it may well be asked and echo from Blaveinn answers 'Why?' That it is much needed is as plain as the cleft in the head of Blaveinn; that it would ultimately pay, if well managed, cannot be doubted. It is not well to disturb the sacred solitude of Nature's great scenes. But we should be reasonable, and if people will go, and ought to go, to see such places as Coruisk, it were better that they should be enabled to do so with some degree of comfort. The true votaries of nature will never grudge fatigue and privation for her sake, but they should not be made martyrs of more than is inevitable. As for scaring away the crowd of tourists, that is hopeless, even were it laudable." Today the Grand Hotel de Pension de Camasunary was just splendid in its solitude, and in its bare simplicity. The twin-roomed bothy may have lacked the creature comforts of the great French or Swiss mountain huts but for many years Scotland's stravaigers have enjoyed it like that. However, they may not get the chance to enjoy it for much longer. Although Camasunary Bay is surrounded by land belonging to the John Muir Trust, the bay itself, the house and the bothy are all privately owned and the current owner has made his intentions clear that when he retires he wants to refurbish the present bothy building and live in it. That apparently is the bare bones of the agreement with the Mountain Bothies Association, who currently look after the building.

Approaching the bay from the south, from the Rubha Ban headland, I was relieved to see the tide was out, leaving a sea-fretted pebble strand with fields of golden rushes eventually giving way to the bare slopes of Bla Bheinn, rising like a massive fin from the flatness of the bay. The old suspension bridge, built by the army, that once spanned the Abhainn Camas Fhionnairigh, is long gone and has never been replaced, so we waded across the shallow estuary and climbed the pebble beach to the bothy. From Camasunary Gina and I took the coastal path to Elgol, a delightful walk on a narrow path that traverses the hill slopes high above the waves. The original plan for our television programme was also to finish at Elgol but I had three major concerns – we hadn't climbed any big hill; that the route to Elgol was too short; and, most important of all, I was keen to visit the cleared villages of Suisnish and Boreraig.

The south ridge of Bla Bheinn

I was also aware that the notion of a Skye Trail wasn't new and it certainly wasn't our idea. David Paterson's book, *A Long Walk Through Skye*, can probably be credited as the first to record a route that covered the length of the island, but I didn't particularly like the idea of finishing the route with rough coastal walking down the Sleat Peninsula to Armadale, as David's route suggested. Instead, an email from Paul Webster, who runs the excellent www.walkhighlands.co.uk website, and who was living on Skye at the time, suggested a new trail that had been built along Strath Suardal between Kilchrist and Broadford, the so-called Marble Road, the line of an old railway track that once ran from the marble quarries at Torrin to Broadford Bay.

Cameron and Alasdair Macpherson of the John Muir Trust

Discussing the matter with Richard we decided that the Marble Road would tie in nicely with the hill track to Boreraig – and give us the option of climbing Bla Bheinn, one I was keen to grasp. The ascent would also give us the opportunity to discuss the work of the mountain's owner, the John Muir Trust. This conservation charity has become one of the prime campaigning organisations in Scotland, a real and effective advocate for wildness. So, about three weeks after Gina and I completed our recce walk between Duntulm and Elgol, our little BBC film crew travelled back to Skye to meet up with Alasdair Macpherson, the manager of the three Skye estates owned by the John Muir Trust. Alasdair is one of a rare breed – someone who is employed as a manager by a conservation agency and who is actually local. Not only that but he's a native Gaelic speaker! There has been ongoing, and sometimes bitter, criticism in the highlands that so many conservation organisations bring in people from the south to manage their estates, folk with impressive university degrees but not a lot of experience of working the land, and folk from very different cultural backgrounds. Alasdair Macpherson was born and brought up in the nearby village of Heast. His grandfather worked on these hills as a shepherd and his mother's people came from Elgol. After a few years working in the south Alasdair was delighted to be able to return to Skye, to the village where he was born. His own children attend the local Gaelic medium school.

The John Muir Trust acquired the Torrin estate in 1991, the Strathaird estate (Bla Bheinn is on Strathaird) and Sconser in 1997. All three estates are of national and international conservation significance and not just for the superb mountain scenery on offer. There is considerable archaeological significance hereabouts. An archaeological survey commissioned by the Trust revealed more than 300 sites dating from the last 6,000 years, containing some of the best documented archaeological landscapes on the west coast of Scotland. Most were the remains of shielings and huts but also identified were several ancient (or 'fossilised') landscapes: land divisions with hut circles, tracks, pens, cairns, piles of stones and other settlement remains. Two of these landscapes were from the Bronze and Iron Ages and a third, in Glen Scaladal, is probably the site of a Viking-period farm (the Norse name Scaladal meaning 'first-house glen'). There is also a rich and vibrant plant life and a very varied geology. Vegetation is limited on many of the higher hills in the area, with some exceptions such as the rare mountain avens, found in limestone outcrops on the south-west ridge of Blà Bheinn. Luxuriant species-rich tall herb vegetation has developed on north-west facing crags and ledges in Coire Uaigneich of Blà Bheinn, accompanied by numerous mosses and liverworts. Central to Alasdair's work on Skye, and something very close to his own heart, is the whole idea of integrating conservation with crofting and other uses of the land, such as forestry.

When the JMT bought the Strathaird Estate the purchase included 1,200 sheep, a flock that has been gradually sold off to allow the natural vegetation and plant life to flourish. Alasdair had been busy rounding up the remaining couple of hundred sheep for the market, a job, I suggested, that must have had a bitter-sweet resonance for him, given the shepherding lineage of his family? He shrugged his shoulders at the suggestion. "We'll still have sheep in this part of Skye, but not on this hill. For example we've decided to give 250 hectares to the common grazing committee at Elgol – this followed a suggestion from the community there. It's particularly important as it's the best grazing land on the peninsula."

As I followed Alasdair up the hill, panting a little to keep up with his long-legged shepherd's stride, it struck me that the only other time I had climbed Bla Bheinn by its long south-western ridge was in the company of another local Skye man.

West ridge of Bla Bheinn from Glen Sligachan

About 12 years ago I had been convinced that the ex-Runrig singer Donnie Munro had friends in high places. Making a programme for the BBC2 Wilderness Walks series we had wandered up the length of Skye's Glen Sligachan, diverting to take in the marvellous Norse-sounding peak of Marsco, a mountain that Donnie had sung about often enough but had never climbed, then camped by Loch Coruisk before trekking out to Camasunary where Donnie announced a desire to climb his favourite mountain, Bla Bheinn. And all in brilliant weather! I had never climbed the hill from Camasunary, and neither had Donnie, but what a superb route it turned out to be. It was a day in a million, with calm seas, astonishingly clear views of the neighbouring Cuillin, and the sustained rocky ridge, with some nice scrambling sections, carried us from sea-level to summit. We sang the praises of Skye all the way to the top, Donnie somewhat more melodiously than me.

"Because the children had been born and brought up deep in Glen Sligachan they had never seen anyone in their lives. No-one passed by, there were no casual walkers in those days."

As we climbed high about the curve of the bay I mentioned to Alasdair that we had walked down Glen Sligachan before climbing over to Coruisk. "Ah", he said, "then you'll have passed what's left of my grandfather's old blackhouse below Marsco." I remembered it all too clearly, the huddle of stones where we'd stopped for lunch and the tilt of green fields gently sloping down the slope towards the river. "I don't know if you've heard the story about the christening at Marsco?" asked Alasdair. I said I hadn't. "It's quite a famous tale, and involved my grandfather. Because the children had been born and brought up deep in Glen Sligachan they had never seen anyone in their lives. No-one passed by, there were no casual walkers in those days. Anyway, the minister in Portree was called for to perform the christening. The father, Neil himself, had to physically drag the children out from under the bed and out from the cupboards because they had never seen anyone before. They were terrified. The minister wasn't impressed either. He threw the water at them, then went back from where he had come from. That's quite a famous story within Skye circles."

It wasn't long before we saw the ragged outline of the neighbouring Cuillin across the ridges of Sgurr na Stri and Sgurr Hain. Deep below us the waters of Loch na Creitheach lay wind-ruffled in the deep clench of the craggy slopes. Not for the first time I thought it a pity that Bla Bheinn dwells in the shadow of its more illustrious neighbours, the Skye Cuillin. While it lacks the serrated, sawtoothed outline of the western ridge it does boast certain characteristics that give it a completely independent personality. Perhaps the most obvious is that the views of the Black Cuillin are infinitely finer than from any viewpoint on the main ridge itself. We stopped for a rest, riveted by the view, and although Alasdair has probably seen this particular sight as often as he's had hot dinners it still obviously impressed him deeply. I asked him what this kind of landscape meant to him?

"Well I suppose I feel a lot of freedom," he said. "I was away down south for a few years so it was good to come home and experience this freedom again. And the freedom you've got here is boundless. When you're working here as well as living here you get a double bonus. I enjoy being out and about. I'm not an office fellow – I don't think you can be in this kind of job. I enjoy the stalking on the hill and I enjoy the forestry work, which is probably about seventy percent of the work I do. It's great, working in the woods, getting rid of the conifers and replanting with broadleaves, getting the woods back to their natural state. I enjoy that, and I can see the changes that have come about over the years already."

As we chatted a golden eagle passed us, so close that we could see the yellow of its eye. And then another, and another… "What a sight," Alasdair remarked. "I think it's the fact that they were so rare and now we've seen three in the space of a few minutes. It's so magnificent, it's still a thrill to see them. You tend to see a lot more sea eagles come in these days although they don't nest on our estates, but they do come in quite often and I see them most days above our office in Strathaird. And the goldens are doing quite well – they're breeding quite successfully."

In a Scotland where birds of prey are still being poisoned on a regular basis it was a delight to hear the excitement in Alasdair's voice, a genuine appreciation of the natural world. But could he reconcile his conservation-minded management of these estates with local traditions and customs, where some people still regard raptors are a kind of lamb-stealing vermin? "I think with any conservation organisation there's always suspicions, especially when people don't know what's going on," he told me. "That suspicion is always going to be there but I do like to think we have good relationships with those folk who live on our estates. You certainly get the odd frictions, or misunderstandings, but at the end of the day we talk to the folk, and they talk to us." "It must help a lot having someone like yourself managing here, a local lad, a Gaelic speaker?" I said. "Yes, I think it perhaps does. I went to school with many of the people here. I've grown up with them. You've always liked them, or maybe you've always not liked them…" he replied with a grin.

Bla Bheinn and Clach Glas from Coire Uaigneich

Bla Bheinn, 928m/3045ft, not only offers a splendid platform from which to gasp at the audacious outline of the Black Cuillin but also gives you the opportunity to appreciate the subtler curves of their pink-red neighbours. The Red Cuillin, north and east of Loch Slapin, and north of Loch na Creiteach, are rounded, made of granite and exhibit a reddish hue. Blà Bheinn and other hills to the west of the area are part of the Black Cuillin and are mainly gabbro, a grey or brown crystalline rock, interspersed with smooth and slippery basalt. Many years ago, on my first visit to Bla Bheinn on a day of gusting winds and racing clouds, I struggled up the eastern ridge and broke the summit ridge skyline just as the wind tore a great gash in the low clouds. Through that hole the sharp peaks of the Cuillin appeared as crooked, tortured remnants of some hyperborean wilderness and through the roar of the wind I could hear something else. It was the cacophony of geese, no doubt disoriented by the racing cloud and the wind. Their music was clear, blending with the gusts into a natural melody that had me trembling in delight.

The most popular route to the summit starts from the road near the head of Loch Slapin and follows the Allt na Dunaiche up and into Coire Uaigneich. An often muddy footpath follows the north side of the stream, weaving its way initially through some heather-covered moraines and a fine gorge. Further on, tree-fringed cascades make a great foreground to the forbidding grey walls of Bla Bheinn, Clach Glas and Sgurr nan Each. Beyond the falls, the path bends to the left and crosses the stream, steepening now as it takes more of a south-westerly line up heather, then grassy slopes and into Coire Uaigneich, the secret corrie, and a very different world.

Loch Fionna-choire lies like a sparkling diamond amid a world of chaos. Scree shoots and grey buttresses dominate, and a line of man-built cairns march resolutely towards the horrid confines of the Great Scree Gully. Ignore the cairns, and instead turn to the right where a rough path takes a zig-zag line up the southern slopes of the east ridge before becoming clearer on the higher screes as it passes the top of the Great Prow which appears on the right. Reach a small top on the hill's eastern shoulder from where the ridge becomes much more straightforward as it narrows and weaves gently to the left and then to the right. Buttresses intermittently bar the way, but pose little difficulty other than some mild scrambling before the ridge broadens out to where the summit trig point and cairn announces not only the top of Bla Bheinn, but the sudden and astonishing view across Glen Sligachan to the wondrous Cuillin.

Beinn Dearg over Loch Slapin

Approaching from Camasunary, we climbed to the hill's south-western top first before negotiating a steep and eroded descent that drops down to the top of the Great Scree Gully, a dank and cold place of moving scree and loose rock. From there it was an easy climb to the summit trig point. I asked Alasdair how important John Muir was these days, almost a century after his death? Has he been much of an influence, or is his name just used as a kind of figurehead? Alasdair thought for a moment, his face creased in concentration. "You know," he said looking up at me, "the organisation probably wouldn't exist without him. I know that sounds kind of corny. You wonder who would own these estates if it wasn't for him and the influence his writings have exerted on those who founded the organisation. I mean he's a very important guy all round, not only for Scotland but for the whole world. He was one of the first men of his kind who advocated conservation of wild lands and I suspect the ideas he mooted in nineteenth century California are probably more relevant for us today than they were then. At that time he was possibly thought of as a bit of a crank, whereas today to certain people he's almost a demi-god! I believe his thoughts and ideas are more important than ever, and we can all learn, and be inspired by the articles and books he left behind."

As we left the summit, Alasdair confided in me that his knees were pretty shot and he might be a bit slow on the descent. After our fast ascent I felt curiously relieved. We decided the quickest descent was to return south along the summit ridge and down to the head of the Great Scree Gully. Beyond it we carefully made our way south from the south-west top which is reached from the gully by a mild scramble, and then followed the broad south-east ridge to the upper slopes of Coire Uaigneich and the footpath down to the grey-blue waters of Loch Slapin.

SUISNISH AND BORERAIG

Map
Ordnance Survey 1:50,000 Landranger Sheet 32 (South Skye).

Distance
20 kilometres/12 miles.

Approx. time
8-10 hours.

Terrain
Minor roads and good footpaths.

Trail Information

Route

Follow the B8083 round the head of Loch Slapin and through Torrin. After Kilbride take the first turning on the right and follow the minor road to Camas Malag. From there follow the old Agricultural Board track S to Suisnish. Cross the fields in an E direction and climb the slopes to pick up the Boreraig path which runs below Carn Dearg. Follow the path over a headland, down a steep gully and along the shore of Loch Eishort to Boreraig. Beyond the cleared village follow the path that climbs uphill beside the Allt na Pairte to Strath Suardal.

Accommodation

There are a number of bed and breakfast establishments in and around Torrin; for details see www.ealaghol.co.uk/area/torrin/

SUISNISH AND BORERAIG

There can be little doubt that one of the great views of Scotland is of the castellated buttresses and crags of Bla Bheinn from Torrin, across the waters of Loch Slapin. One of the more surprising elements of this view is that so many images have been photographed from below a canopy of trees, softening the effect of the harsh mountain imagery and suffusing these photographs with an element of pastoral gentility, not something you expect on the Isle of Skye. Like most of the western isles, Skye is not particularly famed for its natural woodlands but here at Torrin, on the shores of Loch Slapin, we're looking at a landscape modified by humans. Fine woodlands with hazel, ash and hawthorn have survived here and at Kilbride and Leac nan Craobh and along the coast, in gullies and on steep ground where the sheep can't get at them there are other semi-natural woods, mostly on land under crofting tenure. I couldn't recall seeing many trees since we walked through the Braes and after the raw grandeur of Glen Sligachan, Coruisk and our ascent of Bla Bheinn I wanted to sit amongst the woods and the anemones for a while, enjoying the shade and the birdsong before tackling the coastal road to Suisnish and Boreraig and all the barren, bare and desolate resonances those cleared villages would certainly conjure up.

Lying on a bed of Durness limestone, which accounts for the surrounding greenery, there's been a community here at Torrin for over 2,000 years and our Celtic ancestors would have treasured the fertility of the place. Indeed, the word 'druid' comes from the Celtic words for oak tree – *duir*, and knowledge – *wid*.

The view back towards the Red Cuillin from Loch Slapin

The oak has a special significance – it was thought to be a portal to sacred knowledge. Druids also tended to meet in woodland groves and they often slept on beds made from rowan (which was sacred to the triple-goddess Brigid, and used as a protection against enchantment) to try to induce prophetic visions. Hazel was used in much the same way. Druids, who have been much romanticized in modern times, were simply a hereditary class of priests and magicians who characterized early Indo-European societies. They were the Celtic equivalent of the Indian Brahmins or the Iranian magi, and like them specialized in the practices of magic, sacrifice and augury. They were the wise men, the councillors of the Celtic world.

The wood of various trees all had a function in the Celtic world, sometimes practical, sometimes symbolic. For example, the sap from the birch was used to treat rheumatism and, with an accompanying spell and chant or two, was even thought to promote fertility. The yew, even today found in churchyards throughout the country, was associated with death and re-birth. The first three letters of the Celtic alphabet were associated with trees – *Beith* (birch) *Luid* (rowan) and *Nuin* (ash) and when a tribe cleared a tract of land they always left a tree in the middle. The symbolic power of the tree was very important, and it was here, below the spreading branches, that their chiefs would be inaugurated. Here was a connection with both heaven and the underworld – the branches reaching to the sky, connecting us to the power of the elements and the ever-changing heavens, while the roots extended far below the earth to whatever powers the otherworld could provide.

The special relationship the Celts had with trees was recognized by Alexander Carmichael in his *Carmina Gadelica*, a collection of prayers, incantations, runes and blessings, collected from the Gaelic-speaking regions of Scotland between 1855 and 1910.

"Choose the willow of the streams

Choose the hazel of the rocks

Choose the alder of the marshes

Choose the birch of the waterfalls

Choose the ash of the shade

Choose the yew of resilience

Choose the elm of the brae

Choose the oak of the sun"

Amidst the general starkness and rock and water-dominated landscape of Skye, this area around Torrin really is something of an oasis. I chose an ash, the 'ash of the shade', and sat below it, allowing its essence to seep into my own being, expanding my own mind to the skyward reach of the uppermost branches. Did I gain any divine revelation? Was I aware of my spirit being refreshed and revitalised? Well, not exactly. I was still a little bit footsore but it was a great feeling to sit in the shade for a while, at least until the midges drove me on. And it was particularly pleasurable to sit on the edge of some natural woodland looking across Loch Slapin to the magnificent outline of Clach Glas and Bla Bheinn. I don't think I'd ever seen these hills look so majestic, so powerful, the natural embodiment of all that Celtic lore and Fingalian legend. The poet Robert Buchanan referred to it as King Blaabheinn, the mighty one. Mmm, maybe I had been refreshed, perhaps I had taken some emotional strength from the tree – the ash of the shade! As I moved off from the wood, my pack creaking on my back and trekking poles clip-clopping on the unforgiving tarmac of the road, the words of Sorley MacLean came to mind – "The power of beauty, to let us see beyond tragedy."

So often tragedy occurs in the presence of beauty, and beauty in itself is no barrier to the heartbreak and calamity that befalls man. I was well aware that a perfectly good example of that lay nearby, only a short distance from this enduring scene of woodland, sea-loch and mountain, but more of that later. First I wanted a coffee and a scone at the Torrin café and then I was going to meet an old and very special friend. David Craig was born in Aberdeen and educated there and at Cambridge.

With author and old friend David Craig

He has taught literature and poetry and social history in schools and universities throughout England and Scotland, and when I first worked with him he was the UK's first professor of creative writing. He is also a climber and was a guest on my earlier television series Wilderness Walks when he took me to visit some of the cleared villages of Knoydart. David Aaronovitch, reviewing that programme for *The Independent*, described David as an indefatigable walker and talker. "He explained the tragic landscape of the Highland Clearances, with its fallen walls and landscape so beautiful it hurts. I am distinctly fatigable, but I badly wanted to go with them."

David Craig oozes that kind of charismatic charm. Over the years he's created a band of followers – climbers, writers and poets – who all hold him in high esteem. Some have even endowed him with the status of a guru. And it's no surprise that he has enjoyed a long and successful career as a teacher for he has a way of articulating things, whether it's landscape or politics or poetry, that uses language in a precise and quite beautiful way. I first came across David's work in the 1980s when I was editor of *Climber* magazine and he had written his book about rock climbing – *Native Stones*. I was very aware that few climbers wrote in such a beautifully descriptive way, with perhaps the exception of Jim Perrin, but it wasn't until a few years later that the complete breadth of David's skill as a writer and storyteller was realized in his book, *On the Crofter's Trail*.

I'd already had a notion of where David's sympathies lay with regard to the whole question of the Highland Clearances – even in his climbing book he referred without sentiment to the remains of townships in the glens of his homeland, and he was well acquainted with the silence of the glens – but rather than simply regurgitate so much of the considerable genre of writings about the Clearances he did something quite different. He visited 21 islands in Scotland and Canada, clocked up hundreds of kilometres of tramping across moors and through glens to visit the cleared villages and to collect the words of men and women of both countries as they recounted the suffering of their relatives, many of who were far from distant. David spent many years researching the Clearances and he achieved something many people thought was impossible. By delving into the memories of the descendants of the cleared people, he established an oral history of that cruel and dark period.

It was a technique with some precedence. The great Scottish musicologist and folklorist Hamish Henderson travelled extensively throughout Scotland collecting songs and remnants of songs from the travelling people, creating a vitally important archive about a section of society that was in danger of being forgotten or ignored. David Craig was performing a similar service but his subject was considerably more poignant and much more profound. In essence David was collecting evidence, albeit second-hand evidence, about an era of Scottish history that society had chosen to ignore. Some even denied its very existence.

At school in Scotland in the 1950s and 60s I was never taught about the Highland Clearances, a part of our heritage that history had forgotten. The nearest I came to learning anything about forced emigration came from tear-jerking songs sung by wee men in kilts and oversized sporrans. Later, when I became interested in traditional folk music I learned a little more from the genre of Gaelic song, but it wasn't until I began poking about glens and climbing Scotland's mountains that certain questions began to niggle me. What had happened to the people who once lived in these glens, the people who built their shielings here in the summer months? Where did they go, and why? I was well aware that certain places still held an atmosphere of sadness, of tragedy, what I've often referred to in my writing as a 'spirit of place', but what I was experiencing was the effect of a period of history that had been swept from the national consciousness by those who had gained the most from it – the landowning classes. It wasn't until I read a book written by an Englishman called John Prebble that I began to get some kind of an insight into the scale and horror of the events. In the foreword to his book, *The Highland Clearances*, published in 1963, Prebble wrote: "(this) is the story of how the Highlanders were deserted and then betrayed. It concerns itself with people, how sheep were preferred to them, and how bayonet, truncheon and fire were used to drive them from their homes. It has been said that the Clearances are now far enough away from us to be decently forgotten. But the hills are still empty… and if their history is known there is no satisfaction to be got from the experience."

Even in recent times historians like Michael Fry, a one-time prospective Conservative parliamentary candidate, have played down the significance of the Highland Clearances. In his book *Wild Scots: Four Hundred Years of Highland History,* he suggests that in trying to improve the land the wealthy lairds were in fact benefactors, modernizing land tenure through 'improvements' because rising population and the advent of the potato blight made the people's conditions untenable. That may have been true in some situations – like many aspects of society there is good and bad – but the oral evidence as handed down from father to son and told to David Craig in anecdotal form does not suggest that was often the case. After the clearances of Boreraig and Suisnish, the factor apparently put out a circular defending his laird's stance on the matter. It seems Lord MacDonald had been "prompted by motives of benevolence, piety and humanity" because he felt the people lived too far from the church! Such crass hypocrisy is almost beyond belief.

One of the ruined buildings at Boreraig

But even after collecting his stories from so many different sources, David still met resistance after the publication of his book. There are still those in Scotland who claim that memoir types of evidence, whether produced in oral or written form, should be considered with considerable suspicion, that such evidence tended to be "heavy with myth." I'm sure David Craig would be the first to suggest that the human memory can be fragile, and that we should only trust eye-witnesses at least until they have been proved wrong. It's perhaps unfortunate that 'folk memory' is so often misrepresented by its detractors, particularly academic historians. In the case of the clearances from Suisnish and Boreraig however, there is contemporary newspaper reporting that would back up the claims of those sons and daughters and grandchildren who spoke to David, the relatives of those who were cleared, as well as reports collected by the Napier Commission, the government inquiry that was set up as a direct result of the Battle of the Braes and crofter revolt in other parts of Skye. One lawyer, writing at the time to a newspaper about Boreraig, reported: "The scene was truly heartrending.

An ancient boundary marker at Boreraig

The women and the children went about tearing their hair, and rending the heavens with their cries. Mothers with tender infants at the breast looked helplessly on, while their effects and their aged and infirm relatives were cast out, and the doors of their houses locked in their faces. No mercy was shown to age or sex, all were indiscriminately thrust out and left to perish."

I'd visited Boreraig before. It was on a day in early spring and the bleached moorlands, yet to be resurrected into new life after a long, wet winter, spread south between Strath Suardal and Loch Eishort like a waterlogged mattress. Splashing across it into the narrowing glen of the peaty brown Allt na Pairte I'd have welcomed a smiling landscape but then, rounding a rocky bluff, I was stopped short by neat, corrugated fields which pressed a bright green crescent into the cusp of brown hillside that flowed down from the moors above. And beyond the fields, spread out like a map, lay the ruins of the old township.

Boreraig was a village of considerable antiquity. A stone circle stood here, well defended by duns, or ancient forts. And near at hand once stood the little Celtic church of Teampuill Chaon, the chapel of Congan or Comgal. Curiously, despite the obvious ruins, the bracken fronds that have swallowed up the lazy beds and the scrubby sycamores that choke the burn, there was still a lushness about the place. A solitary standing stone exuded its antiquity, and tumbled cottages, tall gables still standing, surrounded a more imposing building – a house and byre, possibly that of the former tenant farmer. Close by a ruckle of stones and boulders I stumbled across the bloated carcass of a long-dead ewe. There was a cruel sense of irony in the symbolism of that rain-soaked and matted fleece, a reminder that there is nothing as inevitable as change. The sheep were brought in and the people cleared to make way for them, and now, in many areas of the highlands, the sheep too are gone.

Boreraig and its westerly neighbour Suisnish were 'cleared' in the mid-nineteenth century. The villagers were sent to Campbeltown from where they set sail for the new world on the Government ship *Hercules*. Many of them died from smallpox. Those who refused to go were burned from their homes. The landowner of the time, Lord MacDonald, argued that the people had wasted good land, and it would be better for them, and it, if they were removed. Once the people had gone, the lands were rented to flockmasters from the south. Fertile ground, which had supported generations of crofters, was used as grazings for sheep. In 1852 a report on the Highland Clearances in the London *Times* concluded with the remark: "It is thus clear that the Highlands will all become sheepwalks and shooting grounds before long." Prophetic words, but what now? Lamb prices have reached an all-time low and few sporting estates, if any, are economically viable. What will the next turn of the wheel offer to lost villages like Boreraig and Suisnish, or those that appear to be holding their own, like Torrin or Elgol?

A rough path picks its way between the villages for a few kilometres through a no-man's-land below the rearing scarps of Beinn Bhuidhe and Carn Dearg on one side, and the salt water of Loch Eishort on the other. The tears of the tides have left their mark here and it's not difficult, in the light of recent Balkan images, to visualize the ghostly lines of humanity, bowed under the weight of their possessions, pick their way eastwards, as they did in 1859, abandoning their homes and fields behind them.

David Craig – well attuned to the sad history of Suisnish and Boreraig

"They extinguished the fire, it would have been in the centre of the house, on a stone hearth set in an earth floor, the smoke going up and out of a chimney hole in the roof, by pouring the family's stock of milk on to the flames."

Like Boreraig, Suisnish lies in a spectacular setting above Rubha Suisnish, where Lochs Eishort and Slapin meet. A leaning plateau of pasture contrasts with the blue of the sea, as delightful a situation as you'll find in this scenically blessed Isle of Skye. But beyond the fields, away from the steep cliffs and its salt-laden updraughts, the husks of former homes, the stone shells of the land, cast a shadow across the sparkling seas and verdant smiles. Recent events in Kosovo emphasize all too clearly the cruel resonances in the term 'clearances'. The words 'ethnic cleansing' come to mind. A track, built by the Board of Agriculture early last century in a token attempt to try to encourage the re-crofting of Suisnish, now follows the shore of Loch Slapin north to the bay of Camas Malag, where, across the head of the loch, the magnificent outlines of Bla Bheinn and Clach Glas rise majestically. I met David Craig here and we followed the old track back towards Suisnish.

It had been a while since David had last been here. The inevitable march of years, and a heart condition, had slowed him down, but as we walked along the old Agricultural Board track towards the green oasis of Suisnish with the outline of Bla Bheinn looming behind us, he pointed out traces of the old life everywhere – he was better attuned to the history of the place than I was. It was also quite obvious he was still very emotional about the things he had heard. "In Mull I met a woman called Mary Morrison, from Penmore Mill near Dervaig. This was 20 years ago, I hope she's still alive. She had been told the story of the Boreraig clearance by her father, a Macrae, born in the 1840s, a boy in 1853. When the factor's men came in, when they cleared out the people and their gear, basins of milk were standing, ready to set as cream to make butter. They extinguished the fire, it would have been in the centre of the house, on a stone hearth set in an earth floor, the smoke going up and out of a chimney hole in the roof, by pouring the family's stock of milk on to the flames." He pulled a face and shuddered. "Putting out fires with milk – it makes me squirm to think of it. You know the foul, horrible smell of burnt milk when the pan boils over."

He shivered as he told the story, not so much at the thought of the spoiled milk but at the symbolism of what the men had done, an act of sheer and utter contempt. "For all the fires of the township to be quenched was fundamental to the factor's men. It must have been seen as a breach of something eternal, a snuffing-out of the life possibility itself, and to do it with clean and precious milk, in a single unholy rite? It was unbelievable." Across the fields, with the lines of the old in-bye fields still visible, we climbed the hill, crossed a fence, and looked back on what once would have been a thriving domestic scene. "These things went on here in Suisnish too," David sighed. "The postman who was here ten or so years ago, Alastair MacKinnon, told me about his grandmother Robertson who was evicted from Suisnish. She and her family walked out, eastwards through Boreraig and further on by the loch-side. He said the estate officers put them out with the usual cruelty, burning the roofs to make the houses uninhabitable, so they wouldn't come back, and pouring the basins of milk outside. Later she told her little grandson that her mother shed more tears that night than they got milk from the cows."

The path between the villages climbs to a grassy headland where gulls wheel and oystercatchers shriek in agitation at being disturbed. The path then plummets steeply to a strip of land that wedges itself between the rocky shore of Loch Eishort and the black cliffs of Carn Dearg. I could sense David's discomfort, he seemed as agitated as the oystercatchers, and made comment about how the dark rock of the cliffs was symbolic of what went on here. "Look at these scarps," he called. "Blackish, degenerate stuff, a coagulation neither earth nor rock." Whether his agitation was emotional or physical, I couldn't tell. Soon the texture of the land changed and we moved from the awkward walking surface of the rocky, stony shore to strips of vivid green turf. It wasn't long before we saw the first of the Boreraig ruins ahead of us.

"That's it," said David, "this is the frontier and it feels like a frontier. That horrible black rock is behind us now and we can see the lovely brown rock again. I think I'd call this the start of Boreraig. There'll be more houses to see once we get up there…" He was right. We stopped and examined the wall of what must have been a fairly impressive building. David was looking around in amazement.

Once a home – now little remains

"It's a while since I've been here and everything is so much bigger than I remember it – this is five times as big as I remember. Look, some lintels are still in place over the doorways and windows. The houses would have been handsome, unusually tall with doors that don't make you stoop. The walls are so well masoned that the massive stones fit perfectly with a minimum of rubble to wedge them – some have binks or cupboard space neatly built in to them. Marvellous…" He stopped and waved his arm over the scene. "This is what I call a cradle of civilisation. You just enter into it and you suddenly feel easy – you've arrived! And there's a bit of shelter, a bit of grass and the sense of calm and wellbeing that comes into you." He smiled, the earlier agitation gone. We walked on, pushing the bracken aside to find some stones to sit on, a gable wall our backrest. It was time for lunch.

Looking back along the shoreline to Suisnish

Today these villages are deserted, but it's not difficult to give the imagination free reign and see how they would have once been teeming with life. People were born here, children played here, people died here – there was laughter and no doubt tears, just like any other village in Scotland. I said as much to David. "Everything was going on here. And for all they knew in the 1840s things would continue going on here. I mean they were building a super track up the hill there, up towards Strath Suardal. And they used to get their mail left under a stone up there for them. They were building a future for themselves and this place was as likely to have a good future as not, as likely as any village we live in today. And then, out of the blue – bang! Who can tell how long they would have gone on living in Boreraig had they not been cleared. By the look of it there was a lot of room, and a lot of arable ground. And a lot of space for beasts, and we know there is good fishing for that rock out there, the Bogha Mor, the big bulge, is still used by lobster fishermen as a landmark. So it's a place that had a lot of resources. Who knows what it would have been like – the manner of the clearances was so harsh that it's hard to think of it."

In his research for *On the Crofter's Trail* David had visited scores of cleared villages throughout the highlands and islands. I asked him how significant were Boreraig and Suisnish in the whole story of the Clearances? "Well, I think there's still so much visible, so much in the way of building, and good building too. And spaciousness in both the places. There's a well-known historian by the name of Professor Eric Richards, an Australian, who said Boreraig was a bleak place." He sniffed in contempt. "Well, that's a matter of taste. It's not Bournemouth, it's not Sauchiehall Street. Is it bleak? It would look less bleak if it had potatoes and oats growing, and kail and carrots… if there were children running about. Richards also recently suggested that the Clearances have 'receded into the distant past' and well beyond personal memory. Hmm, not for Mary Morrison, or Flora Matheson, or Peggy MacKinnon of Heast or Alastair MacKinnon or countless others I've spoken to…"

How emotional an experience was that, I asked? "Oh, it harrowed me and made my blood boil" he said. "At least if their story is passed on we've got some pieces of the lives that were lived here. One of the last to go was Farquhar Kelly – he survived to give evidence to the Deer Forest Commission in 1892 and was the last person to be buried up the hill in the graveyard at Cill Chriosd in Strath Suardal. His friends would have carried him up there, past Cnoc na Tuireadh, the hill of wailing, up and along the track the Boreraig people had built with their own labour. It's so sad, after all that effort, they never got the good of it." With the light fading behind us and rain flurries building up over Loch Eishort, we made our way out to Strath Suardal by that old track. Climbing past the last of the houses David took a final look behind him, down at the sea-green arable triangle of Boreraig, reaching back into the steeps of Beinn a'Mheadhain. What was he seeing in his mind's eye? A MacInnes woman rocking and crooning as her man beats his forehead against a cornerstone of their house? The doors chained and barred? Smoke from the ruins lifting to the grey sky? Lines of rag-tag humanity, making their way over the slippery foreshores to God-only-knows-where, burdened by their meagre possessions and their sense of profound loss?

With a shake of his head, David returned to the track and we made our own slow progress out of that one-time "smiling oasis". It was some time before either of us spoke, and that had little to do with the steepness of the track.

KILBRIDE TO BROADFORD

Map
Ordnance Survey 1:50,000 Landranger Sheet 32 (South Skye).

Distance
7 kilometres/4 miles.

Approx. time
3-4 hours.

Terrain
Good footpath and quiet road.

Trail Information

Route
From the top of the path that climbs up the hill from Boreraig follow the route of the Marble Line NE to Broadford.

Accommodation
The Broadford Hotel: 01471 822204
www.broadfordhotel.co.uk
The home of Drambuie whisky liqueur.

There are a number of bed and breakfast establishments in and around Torrin and Broadford, details from www.ealaghol.co.uk/area/torrin/

Broadford Youth Hostel: 01471 822442
www.syha.org.uk/hostels/islands.broadford

Public Transport

Bus services on the Isle of Skye are excellent. Check out the times at www.stagecoachbus.com. There are regular buses from Broadford to Portree and from both these places to Glasgow. Also regular bus service to Kyle of Lochalsh from where there is a rail link to Inverness and the south.

Traveline: 0871 200 2233 or www.travelinescotland.com provides a comprehensive journey planning service.

Kilbride to Broadford

Walking through areas of industrial heritage in a place like the Isle of Skye is a curious experience. You just don't associate this island of the mountains and the glens and rocky coastlines with industry. There doesn't seem to be a place here for smoke and chimneys and factory noise and you might have expected the industrial revolution to have bypassed the Hebrides, but it didn't.

After I climbed up into Strath Suardal and said goodbye to David Craig, I was completely astounded by the amount of old mine workings and buildings that remain here. I knew there were still working marble quarries at nearby Torrin but I hadn't realized until recently that marble was taken from Bheinn Shuardail, the hill whose slopes stretched above us. It wasn't until I started researching the Skye Trail route that I heard about the Marble Line, an old railway that once ran from here all the way down Strath Suardal to Broadford. I sat down by some of the ruins and tried to imagine what it was like here a hundred years ago when the marble quarries were working at full capacity. I think there was a touch of procrastination in my dilly-dallying too – I was aware that the end of the walk at Broadford was only a few kilometres away.

Outside tourism and crofting there are few industries left on the island but in relative terms I guess quarrying is still seen as a major player, though not as big a player now as it may have been in the past. A Glasgow paint manufacturer, William Thomson Forsyth, started a quarry just outside Torrin in 1960, although there was an existing quarry at the other side of the village, Cnoc Slapin on the shore of Loch Slapin, that had opened in 1951. The extracted rock from that original quarry was used primarily in the production of agricultural lime.

Beinn Dearg Mhor and Beinn na Caillich

Now abandoned, the old quarry and the area around Cnoc Slapin was partially landscaped at the end of 2001. Forsyth was interested in extracting lime and the magnesium-rich marble, which he also ground down for agricultural use. Limestone has a high neutralizing value, which makes it suitable as a liming agent to make the soil less acidic. Its high magnesium content also enables it to be used as an additive for soils deficient in magnesium. Forsyth's market was predominantly amongst the farmers and crofters of Skye, but in 1966 a firm from Portree reached agreement to start extracting marble for building purposes. The white limestone was quarried as a high-value aggregate for cladding panels, roughcasting and ready-mix concrete. Today the quarry employs about a dozen people and it would appear their future is fairly secure. Test bores around Torrin have shown that the Durness limestone reserves total approximately 750,000 tonnes (827,000 tons).

Although the quarrying operation is fairly modern, marble extraction has been taking place in Strath Suardal for centuries. The noted writer and traveller, Martin Martin, who hailed from Bealach, near Duntulm, recorded quarries on the south side of the valley in 1703 and during his 1771 to 1775 tour of Scotland, Thomas Pennant noted that the main altar of Iona Abbey was made from Skye marble. It's also claimed that Torrin marble was used in the construction of Armadale Castle, the seat of the MacDonalds, and possibly even the Vatican and the Palace of Versailles! It was considered the quality of Skye Marble was as good as the world famous Italian Carrara marble from Northern Tuscany, favoured by the likes of Michelangelo. Though primarily a limestone quarry, Bheinn Shuardail stone is intersected with hardened limestone, which has been compacted over millions of years to form a species of brucillise marble. However, probably because of this, Skye marble proved difficult to work and uneconomic to extract compared with the Italian alternatives. Nevertheless, the Strath Suardal quarries continued producing marble into the twentieth century. The Skye Marble Company set up a quarry in the Kilchrist area of Skye near the foot of Ben Suardal, but they had problems transporting the cut and cleaned product to the pier at Broadford. In the early years the marble was taken down the hill to an area close to Loch Cill Chriosd by hand, and here it was cut, dressed and polished using water piped from a dam on the hillside before being transported to the coast where it was loaded on to ships at the old pier in Broadford.

Rainbow in Strath Suardal – the promise of the end of the trail

In the late nineteenth century, in bursts of industrial fervour, all sorts of Government plans and ideas were mooted about creating rail lines on Skye and the Marble Company hoped that one of them could be used to carry their products down Strath Suardal to Broadford, but much of the talk was fanciful and the railway lines never appeared. Instead the company had to invest heavily in a railway track of their own. In 1904 a narrow-gauge line from Kilchrist to Broadford Pier was built at a cost of £30,000, including the construction of a bridge to span the Broadford River – a huge capital outlay for the time. The line was initially operated by horse-power, however this clearly wasn't efficient as six years later the company invested even further and brought two locomotives over to Skye. The Skye Marble Company Limited was incorporated in 1907 and assumed ownership of the quarry. Quarrying continued using a partly migrant workforce – valuation rolls from the time tell us there were twelve local men employed, and thirteen Belgian quarrymen. They were paid about 80 pence a week but at the outbreak of the Great War in 1914 recurring financial problems caused the company to go into voluntary liquidation. The trains were sold and most of the buildings at the former works at Kilbride were dismantled, and the railway soon became derelict. In 1935 some small-scale quarrying was started up again by a new company – the White Rock Company of Glasgow, but war once again intervened in 1939 and the Ben Suardal marble quarry was finally abandoned.

The Marble Road in Strath Suardal

There are still enough artefacts and industrial relics lying around to stir the ghosts of the former industry – the 60m long south-west wall of the Suardal marble cutting and polishing works survives and you can still make out the old railway loading platform. Close by lie the foundations of the former workers' houses and the remains of the quarry workings along with the circular bed of a horizontal winding wheel and the foundations of the limestone crushing plant. Listen carefully through the wind that sighs down from Ben Suardal and you might just discern the creaking of the winding wheel, the crushing of the stone and the accent of Belgian voices…

To a large extent nature has reclaimed this part of Strath Suardal, although a rather manicured and straight-edged path now runs directly between Kilbride and Broadford, following the line of the old single-gauge railway. This was the work of the Broadford Environmental Development Group, which had been constituted in 2000 with the aim of improving the environment around Broadford leading towards economic regeneration within the area. As far as I was concerned this provided the last link in my long walk through Skye, an easy walk out between the Boreraig track and the fleshpots of Broadford itself – the end of the line and the end of my walk. But before that I wanted to visit the ruins of Cill Chriosd, or Christ's cell, a former church that dates back to the seventh century when St. Maelrubha preached from a rocky knoll that's still known as Cnoc na-Aifhreann, or "hill of the mass". It's said the same saint exorcised the monster that once lived in nearby Loch Cill Chriosd – spoilsport!

In an area thick with standing stones and chambered cairns, written records relating to the church only date back to 1505, and tell us that in 1627 a man by the name of Neil MacKinnon was appointed as minister. Apparently he was a man of violent views and was notorious throughout the area for his cruelty and malice. He was no lover of Catholicism and vowed to report the names of *"all the Papists he knew within the Isle"* to the authorities. He only allowed his workmen one meal a day on Sundays because he reckoned they should be resting on the Sabbath! The last church service was held here in 1843, when the congregation moved to a new church in Broadford, and since then the building has degenerated into ivy-clad ruins, surrounded by numerous burial vaults and gravestones mostly holding the remains of the Mackinnons of Corriechatachan. Indeed, later in the afternoon I caught sight of the Coire-chatachan house itself, nestling beside the Broadford River close to the large conifer plantation that guards entry to the village. It was here that the Mackinnons of Corry entertained Dr Samuel Johnson and his companion James Boswell when they visited the island in 1773 as part of their grand tour of the highlands. A rather nice story relates to the somewhat pompous Johnson who, when asked if he was enjoying his evening meal, said: "Madam, this food is only fit for hogs," to which the lady of the house replied; "Then won't you have some more?" This retort impressed the Doctor who later told Annabel Mackinnon that her mother was the wittiest woman he had ever met.

Remains of mine workings

One of the wittiest people I ever knew was an old pal of mine, the late Willie Wallace who used to run the Broadford Youth Hostel in the same era as Harry McShane, whom I'd walked the Trotternish ridge with, was warden at Crianlarich and I was warden of Aviemore YH. This was an important period in my life, an opportunity to adjust to a different rhythm from my previous city-based occupations. Gina and I had two young sons and to be able to be at home with them as they grew up was important for us. The youth hostel years also gave me an opportunity to develop as a writer and as an outdoors instructor. The early writing was produced on an old sit-up-and-beg typewriter I had found in the hostel storeroom, and my early writing commitments were usually carried out in the early morning when the hostel was quiet or in the evenings when I was only interrupted by someone wanting to buy a Mars Bar or a can of Coca-Cola. When the hostel was closed during the day I had the opportunity to take groups out into the Cairngorms, hillwalking and climbing, and ski-ing in the winter. They were good days. The Scottish Youth Hostels Association was a good employer, we enjoyed the work, and I enjoyed both the climbing and ski-ing scene in Aviemore.

It was during this period that I met Willie Wallace. Born and bred in Glasgow, Willie had moved to Skye with his wife Judith and young family and became the warden of the hostel in Broadford. He belonged to that school of working-class wit that produced the likes of the great Chic Murray and later, Billy Connolly – the humour of the Glasgow shipyards. Gina and I frequently visited the Wallaces in Broadford and Willie and I often went out climbing together, usually on to Beinn na Caillich or Beinn Dearg. We were sometimes joined by Harry McShane, who by this time had left his job as a director in an engineering company and moved to Crianlarich to help his wife Jean run the hostel there. All three of us, as well as being keen hillwalkers, were involved with the Youth Hostel Wardens' Association, a trade-union-like organization through which we became known as the "left-wing of the Youth Hostel wardens movement." I had the privilege of chairing the association for a number of years and amongst my proudest achievements was being involved in negotiations with the SYHA for wives to be paid a salary. At that time most hostels were run by a 'couple', you had to be part of a married couple to get the job, but the single salary was shared between man and wife. It was a big move for SYHA at the time but under the enlightened chairmanship of Philip Lawson and the superb management of Jim Martin, SYHA was both visionary and successful. Today, although economically challenged by the growth of private hostels and bunkhouses, SYHA still do a pretty good job and try as hard as possible to maintain some of the smaller, more aesthetic hostels.

The banter between Willie and Harry was often hilarious and I often found myself rolling around on the hill in stitches. Once, in a conversation about world politics we were discussing Idi Amin and Harry asked, "Where exactly is Uganda?" to which Willie quickly replied: "Buried next to my Grandma!"

The ruins at Cill Chriosd

On another occasion Willie went into a dialogue about the first person to be executed in the electric chair. "His name was William Kemmler and he was executed in New York's Auburn Prison on August 6, 1890 – it must have come as quite a shock!" One day, not long after I had met him, Willie and I were just about to head out when I was stopped by his wife Judith. She took me aside and warned me that if I heard a loud clicking coming from Willie I should encourage him to take a rest. Seeing my curious look she explained that Wullie had a pig's valve in his heart, the result of an earlier operation, and when he became excited or over-exerted it began to 'click' quite loudly. I was relieved when we got through the day without any pig clicks but sadly Willie died at an early age – the victim of heart failure. I guess the pig's valve eventually gave up clicking completely!

It was only after many years visiting Broadford that I learned it was here that the English author Lillian Beckwith set her novels about life in the Hebrides. I have to admit that as a youngster I quite enjoyed the books, *The Hills is Lonely, The Sea For Breakfast* and *The Loud Halo* amongst others, but as I came to know the highlands and islands better I realized that her books were stereotypical views of highlanders as inbred and thick, or devious and sly. Written in a first-hand biographical style, some of her neighbours began to believe that the comical characters on Beckwith's fictional island of Bruach were too close to real persons and she was abusing their friendship. She eventually moved to the Isle of Man. I think it's fair to say she is not universally well remembered on Skye today.

In those early days of visiting Broadford the place had a real frontier feel to it. The local pub was pretty rough and the clientele even rougher – fights on a Saturday night were a common occurrence. Things have calmed down considerably and nowadays Broadford has earned itself an air of respectability, with new shops, a 24-hour petrol station, the Skye Serpentarium, a great café/tearoom and a refurbished, almost posh, Broadford Hotel. At least from the front the Hotel looks quite smart. When you leave the Marble Line track and wander down the road into Broadford the first thing you see is the back of the hotel, and it's not a pretty sight! Rubbish is piled up there, the paintwork is peeling from the building and it's hard to imagine this is the same establishment that looks so smart from the front. Established in 1611, the Broadford claims to be the original home of Drambuie, the popular whisky liqueur.

John Ross and his son, James, who owned the hotel towards the end of the 19th century, developed, patented and sold Drambuie as a link with the 1745 Jacobite Rebellion. The story goes that the recipe for the liqueur was passed on by Charles Edward Stuart himself as a reward for the help given to him by Captain John MacKinnon during his escape from Culloden. The local MacKinnon family then built on the brand's beginnings to make it a truly international tipple. They still own the brand today. The original Broadford Hotel was a drover's inn and Broadford had its own cattle market until 1812, when Thomas Telford built the road from Portree to Kyleakin. Veterans of the Napoleonic Wars settled here and writing in the middle of the 19th century, Alexander Smith said, "If Portree is the London of Skye, Broadford is its Manchester."

Approaching the mine working on the Marble Road

But Manchester doesn't have an old pier stretching out into the blue waters of Broadford Bay. I wandered down the road between the ubiquitous craft shops and galleries towards it, drawn on by the sight of the mainland mountains, distant and blue, across the bay. I had reached the end of an astonishing journey, a walk through some of the most incredibly wild landscapes in this land, a walk through history and a walk that gave me, once again, a sense of the potential that Scotland has for long distance walks of this type. When David Paterson published his *Long Walk Through Skye* all those years ago I'm sure he hoped many people would follow in his footsteps and I'm sure many have, but the potential for a Skye Trail is enormous, a route that would bring sheer delight to many walkers and backpackers as well as a healthy economic boost for the villages it passes through. I sat down in the sun by the old pier, put on the stove and as I made a final brew I asked myself a question that I'd asked many times before. Should we be doing more to promote our Scottish long distance trails?

The reed-covered Loch Cill Chriosd

Such trails have not always been popular. I remember sitting in the lounge of the Central Hotel in Glasgow as a young journalist in 1979. I was there to report on the launch of the first guidebook to the West Highland Way, a route that had been approved for development in 1974 and was eventually opened in 1980. The publishers, Constable, were obviously keen to get one over on HMSO, the publishers appointed by the Countryside Commission of Scotland to produce the official guide to the route, and had brought out their own guidebook even before the actual line of the route had been completed. To add some muscle to their presentation the London-based company wheeled in John Hillaby, whose book *Journey Through Britain* had been published a number of years earlier.

Now John was a wonderful writer, a walker with a scientific brain and a huge love of invertebrates, but he was rather blind to the fact that the Scots might have a different attitude to signposted long distance walking routes.

Autumn colours in Strath Suardal looking to Beinn na Caillich

He also portrayed an immense ignorance about Scotland's hill traditions, customs and laws. Indeed, in his *Journey Through Britain*, an account of a walk from Land's End to John o'Groats, Scotland is dismissed in a few pages of the usual clichés about 'bonny' landscapes and drunks. Unfortunately Hillaby and his publishers didn't know their press conference was about to be hijacked by one Sandy Cousins, an inveterate stravaiger and a staunch defender of Scottish hill traditions. Once Hillaby had completed his bullish, blustering presentation Sandy Cousins stood up and tore the whole concept of long distance trails, or 'Ways', apart. "We've never had them in Scotland and we don't need them now," he roared in his own inimitable style. "We have *de facto* rights of access in Scotland and don't need signposted paths to show us where to go, to lead us by the hand. Long distance trails are an English concept that have no place north of the Border."

A tall and rather elegant gentleman sat smiling at the back of the room, a member of the Countryside Commission for Scotland. When Sandy had completed his verbal attack this gentleman leaned over to me and said quietly: "I agree with much of what Sandy has said but essentially he's wrong. The West Highland Way is going to become very popular." The gentleman was none other than the distinguished mountaineer and writer W.H.Murray, and in a curiously prophetic way he was absolutely correct. Over 30 years later the West Highland Way, between Milngavie and Fort William, has become so popular that during the last foot and mouth crisis, when the public was being encouraged not to go to the countryside, the local communities along the route estimated they would lose about £10M in income. Currently some 85,000 people walk the route every year and it's arguably become the most popular long distance walking trail in Britain. More so, outdoor recreation in Scotland has changed considerably in the last 30 years. I suspect Sandy Cousins would have been shocked to learn that some 4,000 individuals had climbed all of Scotland's Munros and that over 160,000 climb to the summit of Ben Nevis each year. He would have been rocked speechless to hear media commentators like Lesley Riddoch and Ian MacWhirter call for all the Munros to be waymarked with signposts!

Following the success of the West Highland Way, three other 'promoted' trails have been developed in Scotland – the Southern Upland Way between Portpatrick and Cockburnspath in the Borders; the Great Glen Way between Inverness and Fort William; and the Speyside Way between Speymouth and Newtonmore. The latter two were set up under the auspices of Scottish Natural Heritage, and not without immense and almost insurmountable difficulties in negotiating access with various landowners. Even after almost 30 years of negotiations and the advent of the very positive access arrangements under the Land Reform (Scotland) Act of 2003, the final stage of the Speyside Way between Aviemore and Newtonmore is still not complete. It's perhaps because of these time-consuming difficulties that SNH now appear reluctant to 'create' any more long distance trails in Scotland, but the organization has suggested in a 2010 strategy document – *Establishing and Promoting a Network of Longer Distance Routes in Scotland* – that it would be happy to support local government initiatives or community groups who wanted to create their own routes.

Despite the current economic difficulties such 'unofficial' routes are not short in number – VisitScotland's website lists over 20 of them, some of which look very appealing and could, with some promotion, take some of the pressure off the West Highland Way which is suffering from over popularity and overuse. Some of these routes are waymarked and described in guidebooks, while others are less easy to follow and require an ability to travel though wild country.

I'm sure there are probably more. Indeed, through a television programme and a book I've been an advocate of the Sutherland Trail, a magnificent route between Lochinver and Tongue in the north of Scotland. My hope is that the Sutherland Trail, and indeed the Skye Trail, may be adopted and promoted by the communities that they pass through. Our launch of the Sutherland Trail was met by widespread enthusiasm – the television programme was viewed by a huge audience, the book has sold several thousand copies and the DVD that accompanied the television programme has sold well throughout the world suggesting that here in Scotland, on the very edge of Europe, we have something that is attractive to walkers from other countries. It's very difficult to ascertain figures on how many people walk these trails, and how much they spend, but there's no doubt that long distance backpackers do spend money in local shops, on campsites and in the pubs and restaurants of the places they pass through. On the 2010 TGO Challenge, an annual coast-to-coast walk across Scotland, I was shocked at just how much money I spent. I'm sure the local shopkeepers were delighted, and at a time of year (May) when the tourist season had barely started. Away back in 1998 Roger Smith, the event's co-ordinator, estimated that the Challenge was worth about £50,000 a year to the communities the walkers passed through. Conservative estimates today would probably put that figure at several hundred thousand pounds.

Whether the greybeards amongst us like it or not, there is a demand in Scotland, and from abroad, for more of these long distance routes, and for more information to be published about the routes that currently exist. Our four 'official' routes – the West Highland Way, the Southern Upland Way, the Speyside Way and the Great Glen Way – are well promoted by websites and guidebooks but what of the rest? As the editor of one of the UK's major walking magazines I had never heard of some of these routes, so what hope does the general public have of learning about them, never mind folk from abroad?

Looking back towards Bla Bheinn from the Broadford road

"My hope is that the Sutherland Trail, and indeed the Skye Trail, may be adopted and promoted by the communities that they pass through."

I wonder if the time has arrived for the creation of a Scottish National Trails Association, an organization that will publicize those existing 'unofficial' trails and encourage the creation, and development, of others? Scottish Natural Heritage has certainly produced proposals that would see them take on this responsibility themselves, but in such uncertain economic times as we currently find ourselves in, I wonder if they would have the budget to succeed.

Beinn na Caillich in winter

Given SNH's rather poor record on long-distance trails to date I think I'd rather see a separate, and potentially more commercial, organization formed to oversee the development of trails in Scotland, possibly liaising with SNH and local government sources for potential funding, signposting, building bridges etc. It could even lobby the private sector for sponsorship of particular trails. But above all it would give a collective voice to those who see long distance trails as a means of encouraging people to get out into the countryside and wild land of Scotland, even those whose ambitions are no more than walking sections of the route on day trips, and those who realize that long distance hiking trails are a meaningful way of promoting tourism and bringing people to Scotland from abroad. This is surely a far more agreeable way of sustaining local jobs and services that the current wind-rush and promises of economic nirvana through renewable energy projects. And if anyone doubts the potential of the economic benefits of long distance trails, perhaps they should have a chat with those who live and work in places like Crianlarich and Tyndrum, Bridge of Orchy and Kinlochleven.

I think Sandy Cousins made some very good points all those years ago, but so did Bill Murray. Times have changed and we're sticking our heads in the sand if we think that our hills and trails are there only for a few privileged hillwalkers. We need to promote our trails and encourage people to use them at a time when industry and many politicians are doing everything in their power to devalue the wild land we have left. As far as most politicians are concerned wild land is considered only in economic terms. If we try and convince them by philosophic or aesthetic argument we ain't going to get very far. I know that from experience. John Muir worked on the belief that the more people he could encourage to use wild land in a recreational way, the more people would love and cherish the land and, in turn, would challenge those interests that wanted to destroy the wildness of the land. We have the foundation of a huge conservation lobby here in Scotland, but we have to do more to allow that lobby to grow and become more effective. A strong economic argument could help, and to grow that economy we need to encourage more people to use the trails resource that already exists in Scotland.

It's always a bit sad when you reach the end of a long walk like the Skye Trail. But in this case the sadness was tempered by some wonderful memories and great experiences. I thought back to our high camp above the waves on the very tip of Trotternish at Rubha Hunish, watching Minke whales diving just off the shore; or walking down the long ridge of Trotternish searching for Iceland Purslane, that very rare plant. I remembered too, wandering down Glen Sligachan with Sgurr nan Gillean on one side and Marsco on the other and that wonderful ascent of Bla Bheinn, surely the finest mountain on this island of fine mountains.

And at this time, at the end of another great journey through the hills of Scotland, I thought of that symbol of the Celtic world – the Endless Knot, the knot that has no beginning or end. It's been described as a kind of Celtic mandala and expresses the Celts belief in eternity, a transcendental state beyond the material world. But to me, as I sat there at the end of my journey through Skye, I liked to think that although I was going forward to new beginnings, to work on new projects and plan new walks, like the endless knot there would be no end to the love and affection I have developed for this Hebridean island. While I was going home, I was certain it wouldn't be very long before I returned again to Eilean a'Cheo, the Isle of Skye.

The Cuillin from the slopes of Bla Bheinn

Gaelic Glossary

aber, abhair river's mouth, occasionally a confluence

abhainn river

achadh field, plain or meadow

aird height, high point

airidh shieling

aonach ridge

ath ford

ban, bhan white, bright, fair

beag small

bealach pass, col or saddle

beith birch

ben, beinn, bheinn hill

bidean peak

bodach old man

braigh brae, hill-top

breac speckled

brochan porridge

buachaille shepherd, herdsman, guardian

buidhe yellow

buiridh bellowing, roaring

cailleach old woman

camas bay

carn, cairn pile of stones

cas step

ceann head

choinnich mossy place, bog

chrois cross or crossing place

ciche pap, nipple

cill cell, church

ciste chest, coffin

clach, stony

clachan township

cnoc hillock

coille wood

coire, choire corrie

creachan rock

creag crag, cliff

croit croft

cruach, chruach hill

cuach cup, deep hollow

cul back

dail field

damh, daimh stag

darach oakwood

dearg red, pink

diollaid saddle

diridh a divide

dorus strait, gate

drochaid bridge

drum, druim ridge

dubh dark, black

dun fort, stronghold

each horse

eagach notched place

eas waterfall

eighe file, notched

eileach rock

eun bird

fada, fhada long

fearn alder

fiadh deer

fionn white, fair

frith deer forest

fuar cold

gabhar goat

gaoth, gaoith wind

garbh rough

garbhalach rough ridge

gartain enclosed field

geal white

gearanach walled ridge

gear short

gille young man, boy

glais burn

glas, ghlas grey, green

gleann glen

glomach chasm

gorm blue

innis, inch meadow, sometimes island

inver, inbhir confluence

iolair eagle

kin head

knock, cnoc hillock

kyle strait

ladhar forked, hoofed

lagan hollow

lairig pass

laoigh calf

laroch dwelling place

leac slab, stone

leathad slope

leis lee, leeward

leitir slope

liath grey

lochan small lake

maighdean, mhaighdean maiden

mairg rust coloured

mam rounded hill

maol, mull headland, bare hill

meadhoin middle

meall round hill

moin, mhoin, moine bog, moss peat

monadh heathery hill

mor, mhor big

muc, muice pig

mullach top summit

odhar dun coloured

ord conical hill

poite pot

poll pool, pit

puist post

righ king

ros, ross promontory, moor

ruigh shieling

sail heel

sean, sin old

seileach willow

sgeir reef

sgiath wing

sgurr, sgorr sharp pointed peak

sith fairy

sithean fairy hill

spidean peak

sron nose

stac steep rock, cliff, sea stack

steall waterfall

stob peak

suidhe seat

tarmachan ptarmigan

teallach forge, hearth

tigh house

tir area, region, land

tobar well

tom hill

torr small hill

tulach, tulachan hillock

uaine green

uamh cave

uig bay

uisge water

Suggested Reading

General

The Undiscovered Country, Phil Bartlett. Ernest Press, 1993. A bold and fascinating attempt which looks beyond the dreams and aspirations of mountain lovers to ask the simple questions – what is the attraction of hills and mountains, and why should we want to climb them?

Hamish's Mountain Walk, Hamish Brown. Gollancz, 1977. The much loved narrative of the first non-stop round of Scotland's Munros. The original Munro-bagger's guide.

Carmina Gadelica, Alexander Carmichael. Printed for the author by T. and A. Constable, 1900. Prayers, blessings and invocations collected by the Scottish folklorist Alexander Carmichael in the Western Isles in the 19th Century

Sacred Mountains: Ancient Wisdom and Modern Meanings, Adrian Cooper. Floris Books, 1997. Another book that asks the eternal question – why do we climb mountains? Cooper specifically looks at the sacred aspect of mountains, where many have experienced a spiritual dimension that has often changed their lives.

Landmarks: Exploration of Great Rocks, David Craig. Jonathan Cape, 1995. David Craig is a man with a heart for the land. This book examines the significance of great rocks, cliffs and outcrops and the influence they have over those who climb them or live near them.

On the Crofter's Trail: In Search of the Clearance Highlanders, David Craig. Jonathan Cape, 1997. The agony of the Clearances and the crofters' epic migration to Canada is the subject of this remarkable book.

Scottish Hill Names, Peter Drummond. Scottish Mountaineering Trust, 2007. A must for anyone interested in the mountain names of Scotland. A fascinating piece of research that also includes phonetic pronunciation of the Gaelic names.

Highways and Byways in the West Highlands, Seton Gordon. Birlinn, 1995. A revised edition of the original 1935 classic. Seton Gordon was one of the great outdoor writers of the 20th century. A walker, naturalist and piper, he straddled the worlds of the regular hillgoer and the professional naturalist.

The Wild Places, Robery Macfarlane. Granta Books, 2008. A superb treatise on wildness. Beautiful and intelligent.

Magic Mountains, Rennie McOwan. Mainstream Publishing, 1996. A superbly researched collection of tales of odd happenings in the hills. Not a book to be read when solo backpacking on long, dark, winter nights.

Spirits of Place, Jim Perrin. Gomer Press, 1997. A powerful collection of essays, mostly on Wales, that describe the spirit of the people and the places held dear to the author, easily Britain's finest outdoor writer.

Biophilia, E.O.Wilson. Harvard University Press, 1984. An eloquent statement on the conservation ethic. Wilson claims biophilia is the essence of our humanity, a state that binds us to all living species.

The Isle of Skye

Skye, Derek Cooper. Routledge and Keegan Paul, 1970. An excellent gazetteer of the island. Indispensable for anyone visiting Skye.

Old Skye Tales, William MacKenzie. Birlinn, 2008. First published in 1930 this book records a world of local legend, folkjlore and superstition. A history of the main Skye families and also the lives of the crofters.

Skye – The Island and its Legends, Otta Swire. Birlinn, 2006. First published in 1952 Otta Swire travels the length and breadth of Skye exploring the islands traditions, legends and folklore. Contains excellent material on Gaelic and Celtic myth and tradition.

A Long Walk on the Isle of Skye, David Paterson. Peak Publishing, 1999. The first attempt to create a long distance trail through Skye. Fabulous photographs and inspirational text.

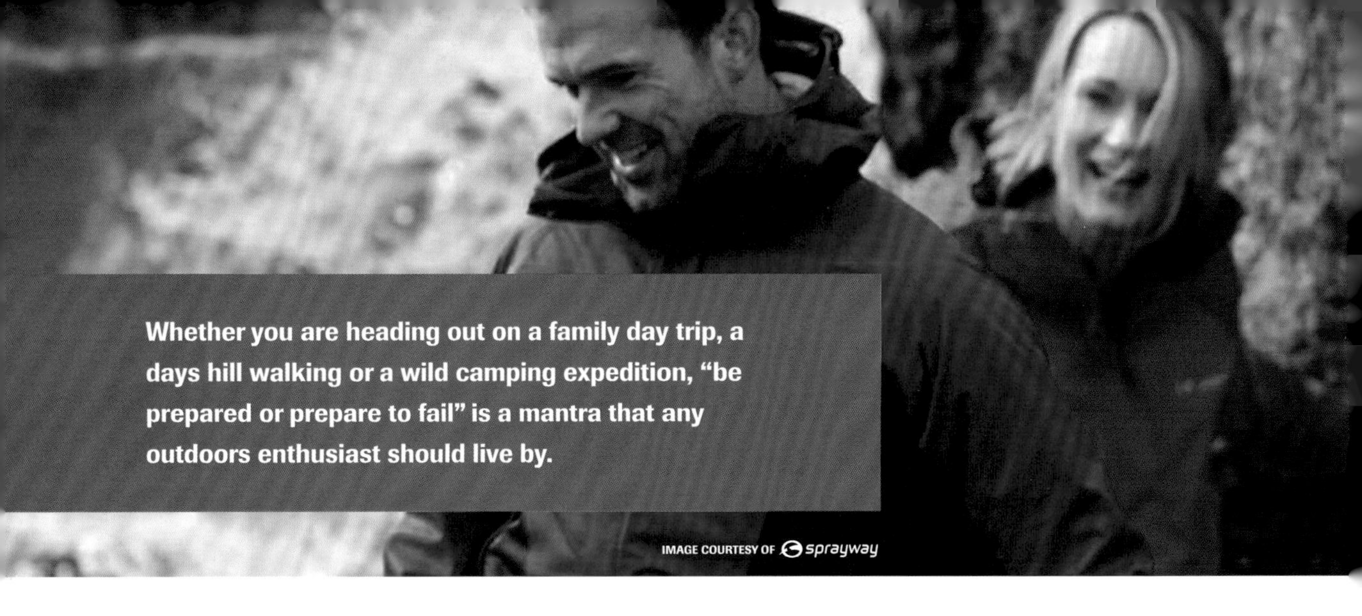

In Scotland top of the list - after insect repellent - is waterproof clothing and footwear. The weather is as unpredictable as the scenery is beautiful and your experience can be ruined in one torrential downpour. The real question is what to buy to guarantee a dry day out? Every store in the Highlands has rails of 'waterproof' items to choose from. The choice is baffling, as are the differences in price - cheap in this case is not always cheerful.

One name that is particularly synonymous with waterproof clothing is the GORE-TEX® brand. A lot of people mistakenly believe that the company makes waterproof clothing. In fact, they make waterproof membranes that are used under license by clothing, shoe and accessory companies. You don't see the membrane as it is sandwiched to or bonded between outer fabrics and inner linings, but don't underestimate the value of GORE-TEX® products on a rainy day in Scotland!

The reasons why so many companies choose to use GORE-TEX® product technology is pretty straight forward – quality and performance. GORE-TEX® garments and footwear undergo the most stringent testing possible to ensure that they maintain the brand's promise GUARANTEED TO KEEP YOU DRY™. Quite a claim, but a proven claim because every element that makes up a finished GORE-TEX® product has to prove its excellence.

In the lab, the garments are put through more stress than you can ever inflict upon them before finally reaching the Gore Rain Chamber where they are battered by the elements. This makes sure that all of the zips, cuffs and seams are waterproof too. Also in the lab, GORE-TEX® footwear is subjected to "walking" in water for many miles to ensure all the components work together to keep water out. The shoes are also tested for "breathability in a special climate chamber. Once the garments and footwear have passed these tests they are sent out for field tests with people, like mountain instructors, whose work puts them in the most extreme weather conditions. This ensures that the products are fit for purpose and perform just as well on the hills as they do in the lab.

So how do GORE-TEX® products work? The porous structure of the GORE-TEX® membrane holds the secret to its success. Each pore in the membrane is about 20,000 times smaller than a drop of water, which stops any water getting in. The pores are also 700 times bigger than a water vapour molecule, which means that sweat and moisture can easily escape. This design keeps you dry and controls your body's temperature.

There are four different classes of GORE-TEX® fabric used in garments and three product classes for

GORE-TEX® footwear each of which is designed for different types of activity and conditions. In garments GORE-TEX® Soft Shell is constructed using soft, warm fabrics and is the ideal choice when freedom of movement is important in sports such as climbing, cycling and snowsports. GORE-TEX® Pro Shell is the most rugged, breathable and durable option and is designed for serious enthusiasts who experience the most extreme conditions. GORE-TEX® Paclite® Shell is used to create extremely lightweight, packable outerwear for activities like hiking, cycling and running, when weight and space are critical. GORE-TEX® Performance Shell is ideal for a wide range of outdoor activities, including skiing, cycling, mountaineering or just walking.

For footwear there is GORE-TEX® Extended Comfort Footwear, ideal for running, trail running and low level scrambling, GORE-TEX® Performance Comfort Footwear, ideal for hiking, trekking and hillwalking, GORE-TEX® Insulated Comfort Footwear, ideal for expedition trekking and high alpine climbing. All of these product classes carry the GUARANTEED TO KEEP YOU DRY™ promise.

Remember- stopping water from getting in your shoes and allowing sweat vapour to pass out of your shoes greatly reduces the chances of blisters – which significantly increases your chances of a great day out on the hill!

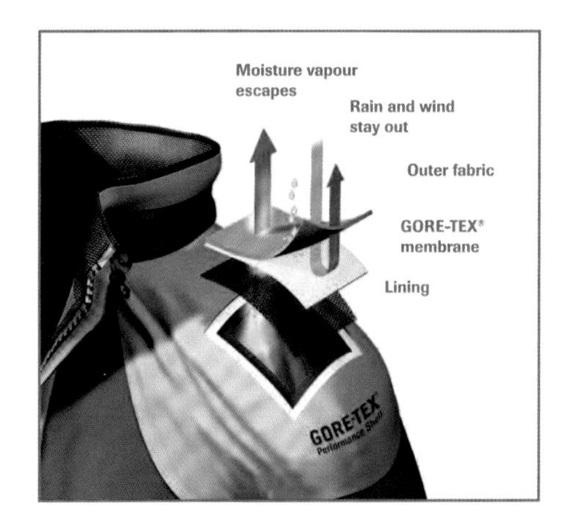

The important thing to remember when choosing any equipment for the outdoors is that you can't control the environment, but by having the right kit you can control its effect upon you. Choosing the right clothing and footwear is just as important as having the right tent, pack or poles and when quality is important GORE-TEX® garments and footwear will not let you down.

Index

MINIMUM IMPACT

A number of years ago, at a BMC dinner, Jonathon Porritt said that if walkers and climbers weren't friends of the earth, then God help us all, but in all the wild areas of the UK it's not difficult to find bags of rubbish that have been left in bothies, water sources that have become contaminated by human waste, and litter crammed into the crevices of cairns and stone walls. Those responsible have been walkers and climbers.

Then there's the damage we do without even realising it. Take a typical Bank Holiday on Skiddaw. An almost continuous line of people make their way up the main path to the summit. Considering the vast numbers who climb up there the path is in surprisingly good nick but the past ten years have seen it widen appreciably and the edges have become comparatively badly eroded. Some of the steeper sections have been worn right down to the bedrock. Spur paths have appeared in places too.

The problem is numbers. These paths were never built for such a volume of traffic, so damage has become inevitable. The Lakeland hills are so popular that many of the traditional paths have become eroded scars and some wild camping spots, such as Styhead Tarn, are over-used and look worn and shabby. Yet the vast majority of folk who walk and camp in the Lake District do so because they love the place.

"Loving the hills to death" has become a little clichéd but it's true, and that deadly love affair has become a growing problem throughout our hill areas.

Much of the damage is done through ignorance. Many people simply do not know how to respect wild country. Some of the ways to minimise your impact are not that obvious and even experienced walkers can do unthinking harm. In the UK little advice is given on how to walk and camp softly in the hills, leaving little or no trace of your passing.

Paths

Hill paths are a mixture of purpose-made walkers' trails, traditional stalkers' and shepherds' paths, sheep and deer trails that have metamorphosed into footpaths and paths that have evolved because walkers have followed each other, usually up and down the quickest, most direct route. Well-located and well-constructed paths can withstand countless pairs of boots, but many paths are neither well designed nor well built and are easily damaged.

The ideal path should be wide enough for one person only, and walkers should go in single file. Walk side by side and you break down the edges of the path, widening the trail, damaging vegetation and creating more erosion and unsightly scars.

Multiple trails – braided trails – through bogs and soft ground mar too many places. Such trails are created by walkers trying to keep their feet dry. The original line of the path slowly sinks under the pressure of boots and, sometimes, mountain bike tyres, and water begins to collect in hollows, forming puddles and muddy sections.

To avoid the expanding bogs people walk round the edges, widening the path and allowing the water to spread. Over time the trail becomes a wide and muddy morass with many bypass trails curving out to the sides.

To avoid this think of the path rather than your feet and stick to the main line even if it does mean muddy boots and possibly damp socks. Where the old path is impossible to find in the deep mud try not to spread out to the sides but stay on the already damaged ground. If you really want to keep your feet dry wear gaiters or waterproof socks like SealSkinz rather than tiptoeing round the edge of boggy paths. Alternatively, splash through the first puddle and get your feet wet. After that it doesn't matter.

Zigzags or switchbacks are often found on traditional stalkers' paths and paths that have been realigned. Such paths are easier to climb and less likely to erode than paths that take a direct line up the hill. A zigzagging path can be a joy to climb and is much easier on the knees in descent than a steep one. However, too often people choose a direct line and cut the corners of zigzags. This damages the vegetation, which results in the soil breaking down and ruts appearing. This creates a watercourse for rain water and soon becomes a flowing stream.

The destructive qualities of running water are immense, so what begins as an innocent shortcut soon becomes an eroded scar. On some paths it can be hard to follow the original line so many shortcuts have been made. As well as ignoring shortcuts you can block them off with rocks or stones to discourage others from using them so the land has a chance to heal itself.

Path maintenance and construction work is grossly expensive and many agencies simply can't afford it. In Scotland alone it's been estimated that bringing all the popular mountain footpaths into good order would cost upwards of £50M. Where path repairs are being carried out it's only sensible to follow the requests of the work party to prevent further damage being done. And when repairs have been completed stick with the new path so that damaged areas can recover.

New paths can certainly stand out like a sore thumb and may initially look worse than the scars they replace but in time they weather and blend into the hillside, allowing the damaged areas to heal.

Off Trail

Going off-trail can be both exciting and adventurous and offers a closer connection with the land. Off-trail travel allows you to go where you want, not where the path takes you, but on the other hand the potential for damage is great. The main thing to avoid is creating a new path. Building waymarking cairns for others to follow is both irresponsible and environmentally damaging. A group should spread out too and not walk in single file, as this could create the beginnings of a path that could steadily evolve into erosion as others follow.

Uncontrolled dogs can cause untold problems. As they range wide they can create havoc amongst ground nesting birds while their owners walk blissfully onwards, completely unaware of the death and destruction being caused by their pet. Dogs should always be kept on a lead or kept under close control. If you have the slightest doubt about their behaviour, leave them at home.

Wild Camping

Regularly used pitches in the hills are all too often very obvious due to the rings of stones on the ground, patches of bare dirt or flattened vegetation and litter sticking out from under rocks. Often there is a network of paths too, leading to the nearest water, back to the main path and off into areas used for toilets.

When using a site like this try not to spread the damage any further and, if possible, try to reduce it. It might seem a good idea not to use such sites but what's the sense in spreading the damage into pristine areas? If possible regularly used sites should be tidied up and any litter removed.

Rings of stones, often used to hold down tent pegs, can be broken up and the stones returned to the nearest pile of rocks or the holes in the ground where they came from. Rings of stones pockmark vegetation and destroy the wild feel of a place and over the years the authors have spent hours dismantling such rings, not to mention waymarking cairns and rock windbreaks.

Often backpackers will pitch their tent on pristine ground. Your intention should be to leave no sign of your camp. First and foremost this means camping on durable ground that won't be easily damaged. Dry ground or at least well-drained ground is best for this as soft ground is easily marked. Such sites are more comfortable too. If your site does start to flood move your tent rather than dig drainage ditches.

A good site is found not made. If you need to clear vegetation or rocks to turn somewhere into a campsite it's better to go elsewhere.

When walking round a site or going to fetch water stick to hard ground if possible and try not to create the beginnings of a use-trail. If you carry a large water container you can collect all you need in one go so you don't have to tramp back and forth to the nearest stream or pool, possibly damaging the bank and making a path that others may follow.

Unless there's no choice don't camp close to water however, camp at least 50 metres from water sources, especially small upland lakes, as you may disturb animals and birds that live there and depend on this habitat. Wild sites should ideally only be used for one night. If you want to stay in the area longer move your camp unless it's on a really durable surface such as bare ground. Staying in the same place for several nights can damage the vegetation under your tent, leaving a scar and a string of little paths round the site.

Before leaving a pitch check nothing has been left behind, including any scraps of litter or crumbs of food, and fluff up any flattened vegetation. It should look as pristine as when you arrived.

Cooking

Campfires are traditional, romantic and potentially very damaging. In dry conditions there is always a fire risk, especially in peaty areas or in woodland, and what dead wood there is should be left for the animals, birds and insects that live in it.

Unless carefully built and sited fires leave scars too, blackening rocks and leaving bald patches of burnt earth. The only place a fire can be environmentally acceptable is on the seashore if there is plenty of washed up wood. Use a stove for cooking and if you're cold don't build a fire, put on more clothes or get into your sleeping bag.

Low profile stoves have been known to scorch vegetation so it's best to find a flat rock to stand them on. If the midges and the rain allow you to cook outside your tent porch look for an environmentally sensitive kitchen site. Bare ground or rock is ideal. Soft vegetation is easily damaged.

Alterations to kitchen areas should be unnecessary. If you want a seat sit on a rock or your sleeping pad. Try to keep the kitchen area clean as spilt food can attract scavenging birds like crows and gulls that may then prey on local species. If you do drop or spill anything it's best to pick it up straight away. It's easy to forget otherwise.

(This applies to lunch and snack stops too. There is evidence, for example, that the crow and gull population in some parts of the Cairngorms has increased in part because of food scraps left by walkers.)

Food scraps includes food that has burnt onto your pan. Scrape this off and into a plastic bag and take it home for disposal. Wash dishes and pans away from water too and dump the wastewater into vegetation. Never bury food scraps in the ground. Hungry animals will simply dig it up and leave a hole.

Sanitation

We are fortunate that we still have clean water in our hills. If we want it to stay this way then sensible toilet practices are essential. What this means is burying faeces and toilet paper or, preferably, carrying it out in a sealed plastic bag. (Loo paper can be burnt but only if there's absolutely no chance of starting a fire.)

Toilet sites should be situated at least 30 metres from running water if possible (difficult in some wet areas). They should also be well away from paths and anywhere people might camp or stop for lunch. Carry a small trowel to dig a hole. In winter an ice axe can be used – though there's no point is just burying excrement in snow. Sooner or later the snow will melt and the shit will still be there. Instead, find some bare ground or somewhere where the snow cover is thin.

The American ***Leave No Trace*** programme is a highly successful project to promote responsible outdoor recreation. It uses a simple set of principles which help minimize our impact on the environment we value and enjoy. These principles include:

1 Plan ahead and prepare

- Know the regulations and special concerns for the area you'll visit.
- Prepare for extreme weather, hazards, and emergencies.
- Schedule your trip to avoid times of high use.
- Visit in small groups. Split larger parties into groups of four to six people.

2 Travel and camp on durable surfaces

In popular areas:

- Use existing paths and campsites.
- Walk in single file in the middle of the path even when wet and muddy.
- Keep campsites small. Focus activity in areas where vegetation is absent.

In pristine areas:

- Disperse use to prevent the creation of campsites and paths.
- Avoid places where impacts are just beginning.
- Protect water sources by camping at least 50 metres from lochs and burns.
- Good campsites are found, not made. Altering a site is not necessary.

3 Dispose of waste properly

- Pack it in, pack it out. Inspect your campsite and rest areas for trash or spilled foods. Pack out all trash, leftover food, and litter.
- Deposit solid human waste in catholes dug at least fifteen to twenty centimeters deep at least 50 metres from water, camp, and trails. Cover and disguise the cathole when finished.
- Pack out toilet paper and hygiene products.
- To wash yourself or your dishes, carry water 50 metres away from streams or lochs and use small amounts of biodegradable soap. Scatter strained dishwater.

4 Leave what you find

- Preserve the past: examine, but do not touch, cultural or historic structures and artifacts.
- Leave rocks, plants and other natural objects as you find them.
- Avoid introducing or transporting non-native species.
- Do not build structures, furniture, or dig trenches.

5 Minimise campfire impacts

- Campfires can cause lasting impacts to the backcountry. Use a lightweight stove for cooking and enjoy a candle lantern for light.
- Where fires are permitted, use established fire rings, fire pans, or mound fires.
- Keep fires small.
- Only use sticks from the ground that can be broken by hand.
- Burn all wood and coals to ash, put out campfires completely, then scatter cool ashes.

6 Respect wildlife

- Observe wildlife from a distance. Do not follow or approach them.
- Never feed animals.
- Protect wildlife and your food by storing rations and trash securely.
- Control pets at all times, or leave them at home.
- Avoid wildlife during sensitive times: mating, nesting, raising young, or winter.

7 Be considerate of other visitors

- Respect othger visitors and protect the quality of their experience.
- Be courteous,. Yield to other users on the trail.
- Let nature's sounds prevail. Avoid loud voices and noises.

You can learn more at the ***Leave No Trace*** website at www.LNT.org.